WHO WAS SHIVAJI?

WHO WAS SHIVAJI?

GOVIND PANSARE

TRANSLATION
Uday Narkar

INTRODUCTION
Anirudh Deshpande

AFTERWORD
Prabhat Patnaik

Published in 2015 by
LeftWord Books
2254/2A Shadi Khampur
New Ranjit Nagar
New Delhi 110008
INDIA

LeftWord Books is the publishing division of
Naya Rasta Publishers Pvt. Ltd.

leftword.com

ISBN 978-93-80118-13-0

First published in Marathi as
Shivaji Kon Hota? in 1988.
First English translation published in 2005.
This edition, with a revised translation,
published with permission of
Lokvangmaya Griha, Mumbai.

Printed and bound by Chaman Enterprises, Delhi

Contents

Publisher's Note

On 16 February 2015, Comrade Govind Pansare (age 82) and his wife Uma (age 67) were shot at as they returned to their home in Kolhapur, Maharashtra, from their morning walk. Their assailants fired at them at point blank range, hitting both in their necks, and fled on their motorcycle. Uma Pansare survived the gunshot. Govind Pansare died in Mumbai on 20 February.

Despite public pressure on the government, there is as yet little movement on the investigation into the death of Pansare. His death is not an exception. In August 2013, when the anti-superstition rationalist Narendra Dabholkar was on his morning walk in Pune, two men on a motorcycle shot him dead. Despite evidence on closed circuit television, there has been no movement in the investigation. The Central Bureau of Investigation has now taken up the case.

Dabholkar and Pansare worked, amongst other things, against the growth of fraudulent superstitions. When Dabholkar was killed, his colleagues in the Maharashtra Andhashraddha Nirmulan Samiti asked Pansare to take up the cudgel. Pansare, a beloved trade union leader and icon of progressivism in Maharashtra, could not say no. The tide of intolerance in his society drew a stiff response from Pansare, who felt that there were connections to be drawn between the harsh anti-worker policies of the government and the growth of ideologies of superstition and magic. Theft of history from the people themselves and the creation of heroes is one way to promote magic. That is why Pansare's book on Shivaji is so essential. It brings a popular figure back into people's history.

Why were Pansare and Dabholkar killed? Absent a real investigation, we might never know. But their murder is rooted in a chain of intimidation that opens with the assassination of Communist Party of India leader Krishna Desai in 1970 — a murderous event that paved the way for the rise of the Shiv Sena amongst the Bombay working-class. Shiv Sena boss Bal Thackeray said of the killing of Desai, "We must not miss a single opportunity to massacre communists whenever we find them." It is this attitude that led to the cavalier murder of communists such as Pansare. The same attitude of intolerance leads to the intimidation of artists and activists who wish to propose alternative visions of our history and our future. There is a line that connects the attack on M. F. Husain's home in 1998 by the Bajrang Dal, to the attack by the Shambhaji Brigade on the Bhandarkar Oriental Research Institute in Pune in 2004, to the routine and unspectacular thuggery against reporters, to the murder of Pansare and Dabholkar.

Who was Comrade Pansare? A lawyer by training, Pansare's main work was to be an advocate of the workers in the trade unions. He was beloved amongst workers in Kolhapur, where he worked hard to protect jobs and ensure livelihoods in adverse conditions. Pansare took on Kolhapur's sugar barons, a powerful force that squeezed the social surplus to their benefit against their workers. The corruptions of capitalism incensed Pansare, who fought against minor instruments of graft such as the toll tax and major instruments of graft such as the impoverishment of the workers. Pansare had a clear sense that the ideological and cultural fight against the Right could not be avoided, since it was in this domain that the Right had corrupted the social basis for worker solidarity. Choking against the pollution of right-wing ideas, Pansare fought to correct the record on Shivaji and on Nathuram Godse, the assassin of Gandhi. When Pansare went to Shivaji University to lecture about Godse, a student activist of the Akhil Bharatiya Vidyarthi Parishad threatened him with legal action and more. In his measured way, Pansare asked the student to do just that so that he could prove that Godse was the opposite of a patriot. He was unafraid of intimidation. In this aspect of his life, as in all others, Pansare is an inspiration.

We are publishing Pansare's *Who Was Shivaji?* as much for its importance as a text of forensic popular history as for a memorial for Comrade Govind Pansare and all those like him who fought bravely and continue to fight bravely against the movements of intolerance.

ANIRUDH DESHPANDE

INTRODUCTION

The Shivaji Legend

This little book has a remarkable history.

Titled *Shivaji Kon Hota?* in the original Marathi, *Who was Shivaji?* is based on a popular speech delivered by one of Maharashtra's foremost Communist leaders, the late Govind Pansare, in Kolhapur, an important centre of Maharashtra's anti-Brahman movement, on 11 May 1987. In his speech, Pansare attempted to put forward a rational understanding of both the facts and the myths around Shivaji's persona and regime from a contemporary, secular and progressive standpoint. It took Pansare eleven months to prepare the book after that memorable speech was recorded and popularized at several places in Maharashtra by the activists of the All India Students Federation (AISF), the student body of the Communist Party of India (CPI).

Three thousand copies of the book were published in mid-April 1988 and the first edition sold out within a month! While the book was under preparation, Pansare spoke on Shivaji at numerous places in Maharashtra including Nagpur, the headquarters of the Rashtriya Swayamsevak Sangh (RSS), and Yavatmal, where the Shiv Sena tried in vain to stop him from delivering his speech.

In Nagpur, the public response was overwhelming. Pansare spoke on two days to a packed hall. The impression he made on audiences in those days can be gauged by the fact tickets had to be sold in large numbers for the Nagpur speeches. Following these sterling public appearances he was flooded with letters, asking questions about and supplying information on, Shivaji. This information, he gracefully admitted in the preface to the book, was used in the subsequent editions of the book. This means that *Shivaji Kon Hota?* is as much his book as it is of the collective effort he inspired in 1988. By the end of 1988 the author had also read, and learnt from, another important book published in the same year called *Shetkaryancha Raja Shivaji* (Shivaji the Peasant-King), written by Sharad Joshi, Anil Gote and Rajiv Basargekar — leaders of the Shetkari Sangathana, a well-known peasant organization of Maharashtra.

The unpretentious logical prose of *Shivaji Kon Hota?* partially explains its immense popularity in Maharashtra. Between 1988 and 2010 numerous editions and several thousand copies of the text had to be published in Marathi to meet the enormous demand for it. In 1988 alone, 11,000 copies were sold in three quick re-prints! Between 1989 and 2010, a year in which 10,000 copies were sold, no less than 81,000 copies were sold. To date, over 200,000 copies of the book have been sold in eight languages, including over 40,000 after Pansare's assassination. Let us also note, in passing, that the years from 1988 to the present coincide with the unprecedented rise of communal politics and the Sangh Parivar in India. Needless to add, the creation, existence and longevity of this modest book has posed a grave challenge to the mythology woven around Shivaji by Hindu nationalism.

In most countries which become nations in history, the great men (and, occasionally, women) of their ancient and medieval past are found standing at the cross roads of fact and legend in the collective consciousness and imagination of the people. This collective historical consciousness is forged over time by writers, poets, historians, philosophers and a media dedicated to nationalism. Ramses, Alexander, Ashoka, Caesar, Changez, Akbar . . . they all overshadow the modern historical consciousness as living statues made of myth and reality. They have all been made representatives of civilizations by the ideologies of nationalism in the course of history and its recording by intellectuals. In time, and due to generations of collected memories fashioned by vested interests and ideology, fact and fiction become inseparable in our love for our heroes and our hatred for our villains. In the haste to identify with the heroes of *our* history and alienate the villains from this process of identification we forget that love and hatred both can be, and often are, irrational. Alexander becomes a champion of Hellenic and Western civilization whereas Changez Khan is portrayed as a blood thirsty marauder in the dominant narratives of history which condition our minds from a tender age.

Shivaji, the founder of the medieval "Maratha" kingdom in the seventeenth century and the repository and radiator of the dominant Maharashtrian historical imagination since the nineteenth century, is not an exception to the tendency of nationalist history, which must seek heroes to justify itself against the enemies of the nation. The copious references to this remarkable man — for a man he was, as Govind Pansare did well to remind us — in the seventeenth century Mughal, Portuguese and English sources suggest that he was seen as a formidable leader in South Western India during his lifetime by his friends and foeṣ alike. Since then his name became synonymous with a "Maratha" power whose rebelliousness against any super-ordinate authority was difficult, if not impossible, to suppress. By the late seventeenth and early eighteenth century, Shivaji's name had become the *generic* name of the Marathi speakers who opposed rising English power on the Western coast of Maharashtra, though Shivaji himself never fought the English, and one of the best descriptions of his coronation are present in the testimony of an Englishman who was a guest at the occasion. English Bombay Presidency records of the late seventeenth century describe the ships and crews of the Maratha navies which challenged the East Indian Company's naval power as "*Shivajees*". Hence, long before Shivaji was transformed into an icon of Hindu nationalism by his *savarna* biographers, he had come to occupy an important place in the observations of the Company officers stationed in Bombay and Surat — a city he sacked twice with lightening speed. By the time the British soldier, administrator and self-taught scholar James Grant Duff published the first comprehensive history of the Marathas in 1826, Shivaji was already a household legend in Maharashtra if not the whole of India.[1]

Shivaji was made an icon of pan-Indian Hindu nationalism by the nationalist historiography and movement which developed in reaction to colonialism and its apologists who asserted that India, unlike Britain, was not in the past, and therefore could never be, a nation in the modern sense of the term. By the time Justice Ranade's nationalist

---

[1] James Grant Duff, *History of the Marathas*, Volumes I and II, Bombay, 1878. The first London edition of this book was published in 1826.

submission on Maratha history was published posthumously in 1900, three distinct perspectives on Shivaji had risen to prominence.[2] The colonial official narrative portrayed him as an opportunist Hindu warrior who flourished in the seventeenth century more because of the weaknesses of his enemies than anything else. Indian nationalist historians saw him as the founder of the Maratha, and thereby Indian, nation — the Hindutva interpretation of Shivaji is essentially derived from this position. The third narrative on Shivaji was developed by the lower caste reformer-intellectuals of Maharashtra like Mahatma Jotirao Phule who portrayed Shivaji as a ruler dedicated to the uplift of the *shudras* in contradistinction to his appropriation as a nationalist by the Brahman scholars.

It can be confidently asserted that after 1826 the name of Shivaji entered the formal pedagogy of colonial education in India designed to promote the "divide and rule" policy of the British. The invention of Shivaji as a Hindu warrior-ruler who had developed a deep-seated hatred for the Muslims in his early life must be credited to the Orientalist colonial imagination of Grant Duff. After this postulate that Shivaji hated the Muslims was laid down, most of Maratha historiography and Marathi historical fiction which developed in the nineteenth and twentieth century, in the words of Stewart Gordon, can be seen as a "gloss" on Duff's master narrative.[3]

Although this is largely true, we must dilate a little on an important departure from this trend in the context of Pansare's *Shivaji Kon Hota? (Who was Shivaji?)*. In 1869 Jotirao Phule

---

[2] *Rise of the Maratha Power*, 1900, reprinted New Delhi, 1961.
[3] Stewart Gordon, *The Marathas 1600-1818*, CUP, New Delhi, 2009.

inserted a discordant note in the Brahmanical interpretation
of Shivaji's achievements by writing a *powada* (Marathi
ballad) on Shivaji which celebrated his achievements as a
Kshatriya Raja in the tradition of a Marathi *shahir*.[4] Phule's
Chhatrapati Shivajiraje Bhosle Yancha Powada describes
Shivaji as an ideal king who lived in the saddle and fought
both the *Yavanas* and the traitors within Maharashtra.
Though Phule's *powada* calls Aurangzeb a "*sachcha harami
shaitan*" ("a real devil"), more because of what he did to
his brothers and father and less because he was Muslim, it
can be read alongside his larger treatise on the caste system
Gulamgiri (*Slavery*) which was published in 1873. The *anti-
savarna* imagination of Shivaji as a sovereign who suppressed
the Brahmanical descendants of the *Yavanas* and elevated
the social status of the *dalit-bahujans* crafted by Phule and
his followers active in the Dalit-Bahujan movements in the
twentieth century provides a part of the epistemological
context of Pansare's *Who was Shivaji?*

In Pansare's terse and admirable book, readers will find
a delectable amalgam of the Marxist and Dalit-Bahujan
perspectives on medieval Indian history, though the late
Communist possibly did not share Phule's perception of
Shivaji as an anti-*Yavana* warrior if the word *Yavana* is
understood to mean Muslim. On the other hand, if Phule's
use of the term *Yavana* is interpreted as a reference to the
savarna Aryan outsiders who were the real oppressors of
the *shudras*, then it would not be wrong to consider Pansare
in agreement with him. From this mixture of Marxist and
Bahujan historiography, Shivaji emerges as an organic ruler

[4] http://marathitheva.blogspot.in/2012/03/powada-on-chhatrapati-shivaji-maharaj.html (accessed on 8.7.15).

of the common people of Maharashtra, broadly called the peasantry or the *shudras*. Pansare's intellectual debt to Phule is illustrated in the following quote:

> Shivaji turned the commoners into great people. They, in turn, made him a great king. Both came together to fulfill a tremendous task.

Shivaji Kon Hota? questions the Hindu communal appropriation of Shivaji as an anti-Muslim Hindu Raja not by portraying Shivaji as a modern secular ruler but by underlining the fact that Shivaji *was* a Hindu Raja but being a Hindu Raja in the nineteenth century did not necessarily mean being a Hindu communal ruler dedicated to the destruction of Islam. How else is the employment of Muslims in large numbers by Shivaji in his navy and other services to be explained? If Shivaji was committed to the extirpation of Islam in India why did he get Afzal Khan buried with full military honors after slaying him in 1659 and sanction funds for the upkeep of his tomb? Shivaji treated Muslims and Islam with respect and was not averse to establishing relations with those Hindus who had converted to Islam and wished to re-convert to Hinduism; no Nazi-style final solutions to the fluidity and co-existence of religious identities were to be found in the seventeenth century. Religion was important to pre-colonial Indians like it was to all pre-modern societies in general, but unlike sixteenth-century Europe, the wars of religion were not to be found in India.

There are numerous questions which make the annexation of the memory of Shivaji by communal historiography to the cause of communal politics problematic. Conceptually speaking, if communalism was absent in medieval India how could the majority of Indian rulers have been communal? Shivaji's attitude even towards the Europeans was not governed by a frog-in-the-well approach which is the hallmark of religious nationalism. He was happy to take Portuguese assistance when it came to developing his artillery and building his forts. Even the sword which he is said to have used regularly was forged by the Portuguese whose military reputation in India during the seventeenth century was quite high; Pansare dilates a little on this in the context of the Goddess Bhavani myth associated with Shivaji's sword. In the light of these facts it is perhaps apt to describe Shivaji as a kind of "equal opportunity employer" in the seventeenth century.

In matters of statecraft Shivaji can be compared with Frederick the Great of Prussia who once famously declared that he would welcome the Turks and build them their mosques if they proved valuable to the Prussian State. Many questions arise in relation to the Maratha-Muslim military and administrative relations which were important to the history of the Deccan in the eighteenth century. Muslims fought in large numbers in the "Maratha" armies during the seventeenth and eighteenth centuries only to be exiled from Maratha history due to the painstaking efforts of the modern historians of Maharashtra during the colonial period. The Shaniwarwada, the intrigue ridden palace of the Peshwas in Pune, was garrisoned by the *Gardis* — the European trained Afghan Guard Battalion. The Marathas fought and negotiated with the Nizam over the *subedari* of the Deccan without speaking of establishing a Hindu *Pad-Padshahi* in the region. The Maratha-Muslim military co-operation continued in the nineteenth century and was demonstrated in the desperate resistance offered to the British by the Afghans in the service of the Rani of Jhansi from within the besieged Jhansi fort in 1857. *Shivaji Kon Hota?* recounts the role which numerous Muslim commanders played in Shivaji's armed forces. There were at least 13 major Muslim commanders or soldiers in Shivaji's army: Siddhi Hilal, Daulat Khan, Ibrahim Khan, Kazi Haider, Siddi Ibrahim, Siddi Wahwah, Noorkhan Beg, Shama Khan, Hussain Khan Miyani, Siddi Mistri, Sultan Khan, Dawood Khan and Madari Mehetar.

Shivaji Kon Hota? questions the way in which dominant Maratha historiography has enforced modern, i.e., colonial and post-colonial, religious categories on a past where people lived and did things differently compared with the age of modernity. Readers will not fail to notice the ease and humility with which the late Govind Pansare has raised and answered these questions. He does not claim originality, but only the ability to rationally re-interpret the facts of Shivaji's career, for *facts* do exist — despite the claims of contemporary intellectual fashion to the contrary. *Shivaji Kon Hota?* shows how, with the help of reason, anyone can interrogate the past. We need not be scientists and historians to discover and understand ourselves by questioning the familiar tropes of history.

What made the book such a bestseller? It addresses an important issue of Maratha history. It tries to, and perhaps successfully does, understand the causes of Shivaji's immense popularity in Maharashtra. It combines Marxist class analysis with the interpretation of Shivaji developed by Phule mentioned above to explain the popularity of Shivaji. The popularity of Shivaji endured in the eighteenth century and left the Brahman Peshwas with no choice but to derive political legitimacy from his descendants in Satara — all new Peshwas had to travel to Satara to get their appointment and the robes. The Peshwa was the *de facto* head of the Maratha state in the eighteenth century, but despite the enormous concentration of financial and military powers in his hands, could not dare become the *de jure* ruler of the state. Why did this state of affairs come to prevail in Maharashtra? The answer to this question must be sought in the way Shivaji dealt with the class and caste contradictions in seventeenth-century Maharashtra. Shivaji belonged to an elite military family but his power rested on various sections of the peasantry whose affections he gained by curbing the power of the *saranjamshahi* jagirdari feudal ruling class of Maharashtra — the oppressor-in-chief of the peasants. Shivaji took several steps to reduce the power of the *Patils* and *Deshmukhs* and other sections of the *watandar* and *inamdar* class and enhance the sovereignty of his state in the overall interest of the oppressed in Maharashtra. In sum, he was politically wise and became a king dedicated to the welfare of his subaltern subjects. This may sound a little romantic but in the light of the facts presented in Pansare's book we are compelled to place Shivaji in the line of many medieval rulers who took the welfare of their common subjects seriously. These rulers were alert to the fundamental principle of paternal sovereignty, which resided in the affection of their common subjects. *Shivaji Kon Hota?* reiterates that the Brahmans of Maharashtra, and even the so-called 96 *kuli* (clan) blue-blooded Marathas, refused to recognize Shivaji and the Bhonsle clan either as Maratha or Kshatriya. This refusal to accord Shivaji the political legitimacy rightfully claimed by him brought into Maratha history the role of the Paithani Brahman Gaga Bhatt who provided Shivaji the Mewar genealogy and came all the way from Varanasi to perform the rituals for the Raja's coronation as a Chhatrapati. The colonial and post-colonial appropriation of Shivaji and his legacy by the intellectual descendants of the *saranjamshahi* class are presented in relief against these facts by Pansare in a language shorn of academic verbiage.

The list of the lower castes whose support was essential to Shivaji's rise to political sovereignty is long. Right from the time when Shivaji, as a youth, began mixing with the wiry enterprising hill folk of the Sahyadari mountains and started his military adventures a number of *shudra* and *ati-shudra jatis* supported him. The *Navis, Berads, Ramoshis, Kolis, Sonkolis, Bhandari* and even large numbers of lower-caste Muslim converts formed the social base of Shivaji's political independence from the refractory *watandars*. We also know that the *Kunbis* and *Gujjars* flocked to his standard in large numbers; one of his famous generals was Kudtoji Gujar renamed Prataprao Gujar by him. Prataprao's daughter was married to Shivaji's second son Rajaram after the general's death in a fatal cavalry charge in February 1674. Would popular support have come his way had Shivaji reconciled himself to the life of a *saranjamshahi* jagirdar living off the fat of the land? Many of the lower castes, and especially the *Ramoshis*, who supported Shivaji were the ones who suffered the most in a Maharashtra ruled by the Brahman Peshwa in the eighteenth century. The increased marginalization of some of these castes under the *shastric* rule imposed on the region by the Peshwai most probably forced them into a life of crime, making it easy for the Peshwa administration, and later the British, to categorize them as criminal tribes deserving of stern treatment. Testimonies collected from some *Ramoshi Naiks* by Britsh ethnographers in the early nineteenth century speak of the *Ramoshi* association with Shivaji and their subsequent degradation by the Peshwas.[5] The *Ramoshis* claimed to have handed over several forts to Shivaji during the early phase of his career — a good turn the future Chhatrapati did not forget.

Unfortunately for the lower castes, the state established by Shivaji did not last very long after his death and the jagirdari class he had suppressed reasserted its power during the period of the *Peshwai*. In fact the *Peshwai* undid what Shivaji had accomplished in the seventeenth century and re-established the dominance of the *saranjamshahi* class in Maharashtra with great force. From *Shivaji Kon Hota?* we come to know that the state set up by Shivaji created numerous opportunities for the upward social mobility of the lower castes denied them by the traditional caste system of India. Consequently these acts of Shivaji became part of Maharashtra's folklore, which was often submerged in the din of nationalism which resounded in the modern middle class narratives of medieval India.

More than a century after Phule first questioned the Brahman appropriation of Shivaji to the cause of a largely *savarna* hegemonic nationalism, Pansare wrote *Shivaji Kon Hota?* to separate the facts from the fictive biographies

---

[5] For more on this see Alexander Mackintosh, *An Account of the Origin and Present Condition of the Tribe of the Ramoossies Including the Life of the Chief Omiah Naik*, Bombay, 1833, and P. W. Bradbeer, 'The Role of the Kingdom of Satara in Suppressing Deccan Bunds, 1812-1832', in A. R. Kulkarni and N. K. Wagle (eds.), *Region, Nationality and Religion*, Popular Prakashan, Mumbai, 1999, pp. 58-68.

of Shivaji which comprise the dominant narrative of that admirable seventeenth century ruler. This book is a Marxist deconstruction of the dominant narrative of Shivaji to which most Indians have become accustomed since the nineteenth century. The strength and popularity of *Shivaji Kon Hota?* must be perceived in it *not* being a product of professional history. It is a modern text not tainted by the historical imagination of nationalism. The book's lasting relevance, readers will realize, lies in its unostentatious application of reason and the historical method of Marx to a highly emotive subject of Indian history.

Govind Pansare has fallen in the line of duty, victim of an assassin's bullets, but his text will live long, a blazing testimony to the power of reason and rationality.

The King with a Difference

Shivaji (1627-1680) is everywhere. Short stories, novels, plays, tamashas, songs, ballads, histories, biographies, films, lectures, speeches — Shivaji dominates the Marathi imagination like almost no one else. Despite this, one cannot say that the image of Shivaji and his times that emerges from this bounty and is imbedded in the popular imagination is consistent with the historical truth.

TO PRAISE A KING IN A DEMOCRACY!

Feudalism, the soil of Shivaji and his times, is an obsolete social system. Shivaji belonged to feudal times. He was a king of a feudal Kingdom. Our country — like the entire world — has overthrown this system. People fought to abolish feudalism. Kings and lords were rightly thrown into the dustbin of history. It was also correct that we replaced these kings and lords by democracy. What happened to Shivaji after his death proves that feudalism was not a system that could be accepted or continued. The Indian feudal order could not stand up to the dynamism of British capitalism. Feudalism's failures show that, as a social system, it is dispensable and worth rejecting.

Should a king be revered in a democracy? What is there in a king's thinking, his practice and his life, for his memory to inspire us in this democratic age?

There have been many kings in history. But these others do not all remain in our memory. Nobody celebrates the birth or death anniversaries of these kings. Perhaps their successors honour them. It is also possible that in some places people of the area belonging to the erstwhile "princely states" celebrate such days. However, such activities are not as widespread and not as enthusiastic as those that related to Shivaji. Why should this be so? What was so different about this king?

How did Shivaji differ from other kings, and from his contemporary kings? To comprehend Shivaji's uniqueness, we need to unlock the secret of his life and times.

FOUNDER OF A STATE

A king who inherits sovereignty does not have to do anything to earn it. He merely is born and succeeds to his legacy. There is nothing admirable about that. Most kings become regal by sheer birthright. Shivaji did not inherit his throne. He was not one of those kings. He founded a new state. It is never easy to found a state — more difficult in Shivaji's case. Yet, he did it. There is a great difference between ascending to a pre-existing throne and creating a new one by one's own efforts.

When Shivaji founded his state, his contemporaries were not even thinking about such a thing; let alone bring it into reality. A common mission was to earn a place in the court of this or that emperor and king and to serve them loyally. The point was to sell one's honour and win their confidence. In this context, Shivaji thought of establishing an independent state, ruled by him. He made a proper plan for his ambition, implemented that plan and finally founded a state.

Of course, Shivaji was not the only one to found a state (and nor did he found this state by himself). There were some others. But even those others have not earned — as Shivaji has — such pride of place in the hearts of people.

"OUR MISSION-OUR STATE"

What is the difference between the work and the state of Shivaji and other kings? The *ryots*, the common men and women, believed that Shivaji had taken up *their* mission and that he had founded *their* state. How does one test whether a state is good or bad? The best state is that which the common people, the majority of the people living under that state, believe it to be so.

We live in a democracy. There are many other democratic countries. Do the people — at least the majority — believe that these are their own states? Do the majority of people believe that what is taking place in their countries is for their good? For me, the honest answer is no! Although these are democracies elected by people, the people are not convinced that whatever is happening in the name of democracy is done in their interest.

There is a good definition of modern state: a state is one that "emerges from people but is also increasingly alienated from them."

Today's democratic state has emerged out of popular struggle and it is increasingly getting alienated from them. Of course, this is not to claim that the feudalism of Shivaji's time was more progressive than our democracy. Three and a half centuries separate us from those times. Feudalism is useless for us. Really-existing democracy is equally of little use to the common people.

INSPIRING SELF-SACRIFICE

The *ryots* of Shivaji's time believed that the work undertaken by him was their own work. They identified themselves with his mission. There are innumerable instances that show this.

In 1660, Siddi Jauhar and Fazal Khan, with a huge army and armory, had laid siege to the Fort Panhala. The noose was not loosened even a bit after months. Netaji Palkar, with the help of Siddi Hilal, attempted to break the siege. The attempt was frustrated. Shivaji's General and Chief of Army had to retreat, badly beaten. The loyal Siddi Hilal, who had tried to save his son, had fallen into the enemy's hands. Shivaji, trapped in the siege, could not find a way out. A plan was hatched to use the smallest of a chink in the siege to escape away to Fort Vishalgadh. A double of Shivaji would distract the troops that encircled Panhala. He sat in a palanquin and — as expected — was captured. Siddi Jauhar, the leader of the army that encircled Shivaji, had no idea that the real Shivaji had escaped. He thought he had him in custody.

Shivaji's double was an impoverished barber named Shiva, who very well knew his fate when Siddi Jauhar's men would capture him. He knew beyond doubt that Siddi Jauhar would kill him. Yet, he took Shivaji's place. As expected, he was captured and executed.

Shiva the Barber embraced his death with open eyes. He had no hope of earning a reward — of, for instance, becoming a landlord. He firmly believed that even if he must die, Shivaji must live. Shivaji's cause was his own cause. It was the *ryots'* cause. Shiva the Barber must have been convinced of this; he was not alone in such conviction.

Shivaji escaped from Panhala. Siddi Jauhar was alerted and chased Shivaji. The fate of Shivaji would have certainly been doomed had Siddi caught up with him before he had reached Fort Vishalgadh. Siddi Jauhar's men had to cross a pass at Ghodkhind. Baji Prabhu Despande and a handful of *mavlas* (Maratha soldiers) stood guard at the pass. They were prepared to die in order to give Shivaji enough time to reach Fort Vishalgadh. This is just what happened. Baji Prabhu fell and several *mavlas* were massacred. The names of these brave ones are unknown.

Why did Baji Prabhu and those handful of anonymous *mavlas* fight to the death? They shared the conviction of Shiva the Barber: They would embrace death so that Shivaji would live and fulfill his mission. It was such a noble mission that they felt happy to sacrifice themselves for it. That was the strength of their conviction.

The escape from Panhala is not the only instance that shows us the loyalty that Shivaji's cause produced.

In 1665, Shivaji conceded defeat against the armies of Mirza Raja Jai Singh, a satrap of the Emperor Aurangzeb. Mirza Raja Jai Singh forced Shivaji to sign the humiliating Treaty of Purandar — not only did he have to surrender forts and money, but he had to send his son Sambhaji to serve the Mughal regime. Shivaji went to Agra the next year to present himself to Aurangzeb. The Emperor's men arrested Shivaji and threw him in prison. No escape from his confinement seemed possible. Once more, Shivaji thought of a clever idea. One of his loyalists pretended to be him, and lay in bed while another loyalist massaged his feet. Before the guards could figure out who was whom, Shivaji escaped. The plot was designed in such a way that Shivaji would get enough time to get away as far as possible before the act of his disappearance came to light.

Who were those who chose to remain behind, to face certain death? They were Madari Mehtar and Hiroji Farjand. It was more than certain that the plot would eventually be revealed. Were Madari and Hiroji not aware that they would be arrested and killed ruthlessly? Of course, they were. Yet, why were they prepared to embrace death? Once again, the same answer. The task undertaken by Shivaji was invaluable. It had to be successfully completed; it had to be sustained. Whatever sacrifice was required, they would make it.

Shivaji performed a miracle, which made his followers believe that his life was more important than theirs. They might die for his life. Other kings could not perform this miracle. Of course, it was not that there were not many who fought for those kings. Certainly, many died fighting for those kings. But they died to earn wealth or a fiefdom, or both. Theirs was not a sacrifice for a noble cause.

Not only did warriors participate in Shivaji's mission. More importantly, the common *ryots* — peasants — did their bit for a greater cause. When *ryots* participate in a cause, that cause is certain to succeed. It succeeds because it no longer remains the cause of a king alone. It becomes the common cause of all.

When people participate, then only can *Swaraj* [self-rule] emerge. This historic truth is recorded in a ballad, whose direct appeal is captured in simple language: "Be warned. A gallop ahead, and I finish you in smithereens…" The bard sings of an insignificant incident during a time of great commotion. Soldiers are on high alert. Even peasants, tilling their land, are vigilant. They watch the soldiers as they pass by. Whose camp do they belong to? If anyone is seen to sabotage the great cause of *Swaraj*, that person will be confronted. Four riders are about to cross the fence. It is at this instant that a boy of a tender age, 10-12 years of age (still green behind the ears!), accosts them and warns, "Halt! Otherwise, I'll cut you into pieces. Who are you? Where are you going?" This young man challenges the armed cavalrymen. Fear doesn't touch him. He too believes that he must do this. This is my job. Raja Shivaji is doing something good, I must take part in it. The bard will later reveal in the poem that the soldier to whom the boy addresses himself is none other than Shivaji. The boy has never seen Shivaji before. He does not know the king. He does not know what it means to lend a helping hand to Shivaji. Yet, he does it, ignoring the obvious threat.

Shivaji generated such feelings amongst his colleagues, his soldiers and the *ryots*. This is the difference between Shivaji and the other kings.

Extraordinarily heroic deeds are performed while fighting to attain extraordinary goals. History does not care to record those who die for selfish goals of earning estates. Small and big people perform heroic deeds in the commotion of battle. Inebriated with war cries, they even embrace death. Such deeds might be done to earn fiefdom or to protect it. But to embrace death consciously, knowing that it is not going to fetch a penny: that is a deed of a different order.

None dispute that Shivaji's companions and his *ryots* selflessly participated in his mission. Not even an iota of doubt could be raised about the fact that this *ryots* held dear to their heart Shivaji's work and his rule. They saw this as their own work and their own rule.

But, how could this happen? What exactly had Shivaji done so that his *ryots* came to believe in his cause? His contemporaries or any such kings of his times could not earn this kind of loyalty amongst the *ryots*. The real question is: How did Shivaji earn it?

The answer to this question lies in the way Shivaji treated his subjects, the way in which he approached the *ryots*. He greatly differed in this from his contemporary kings.

LANDLORDISM AND THE VILLAGE SYSTEM

In feudal times, the common people hardly cared who the king was. It did not matter to them who controlled the territory and who wore the throne. This was simply because no matter who king, the daily life of the *ryots* remained unchanged.

Villages were almost self-sufficient. The village had its own autonomous system. It had a Patil [chief], Kulkarni [accountant], and twelve kinds of *balutas* [servants]. These people drove this cart called the village. They formed the institutional system of the village. Changes in rulers did not affect the cycle of village life. The officers collected taxes without any restraint. They exploited the *ryots*. Nobody listened to the *ryots'* pleas against the injustice by these officers. The *ryots* eventually learned not to complain because they knew none of the officers listened to them, and the kings were absent. The rulers changed, but Kulkarnis, Patils, Landlords, Deshmukh [district chief] and Jagirdars [feudal lord] remained firmly in place. They never changed.

Overnight they might change their loyalties. The slogan, "The king is dead. Long live the king!" was nowhere truer than in their case. They would hasten to the foot of the victorious king to lay down their loyalty. In return they would ensure that their position as officers was kept intact. They continued oppressing the *ryots*, squeezing them for taxes, and filling the king's coffers. The *ryots* only knew exploitation. Why on earth would they be bothered which king's coffers were being filled with the wealth looted from them?

The *ryots* firmly believed that the kings were looters. They therefore did not distinguish between one king and another. The great historian V. K. Rajwade writes in his introduction to *Mahikavatichi Bakhar*,

> All the rulers of Hindustan, over the last three thousand years, whether indigenous or foreigners, were selfish thieves and plunderers and the Hindu populace honestly believes in its heart of hearts, all these kings and governments are nothing but parasites and bands of robbers.

Those who were perpetually subjected to theft were least bothered about who was the thief or which caste he belonged to. A king came and a king went. It made no difference to the *ryots*.

Marx studied Indian social reality in a far corner of the world, in Britain. Despite the paucity of sources before he, he came to the same conclusion. Marx wrote to his great friend, Engels, on 14th June 1853, approvingly quoting a parliamentary report:

> . . . although the villages themselves have been sometimes injured, and even desolated by war, famine and disease; the

same name, the same limits, the same interests, and even the same families, have continued for ages. The inhabitants give themselves no trouble about the breaking up and division of kingdoms, while the village remains entire, they care not to what power it is transferred, or to what sovereign it devolves. Its internal economy remains unchanged.

There was no organic relation between the king and the *ryots*. The king's religion in no way affected the life of the *ryots*. Even if the rulers changed, they adopted the existing systems and continued exploiting the people. The king did not care a damn even though his feudatories exploited, looted and tortured the *ryots*. He was least bothered about such acts. As long as the feudatories paid their revenues regularly, all was well in his kingdom!

Shivaji began work in this kind of social order. His reign established instant changes. A link was established between the king and his *ryots*. The *ryots* could see their king with their own eyes: he was close to them; he met them, he enquired after them, he was alert to allegations of injustice and torture. He exercised power to help them.

The new king reined in the various feudatories. The Jagirdars, Deshmukhs, Vatandars [landholders], Patils, and Kulkarnis could no longer commit their previously unrestrained acts of omission and commission. Shivaji told the *ryots* that the feudatories were the servants of the state and not its masters. Now they came under the king's control. Rules and regulations were introduced regarding what they should do and what they should not do.

The *ryots* developed courage to seek justice in case the feudatories persecuted and tortured them. Their confidence grew as the state conducted enquiries of arrogant officers and feudatories. If anyone was found guilty, the state meted out punishments. These were so drastic that the officers and feudatories no longer resorted to their heinous ways of subjecting the *ryots* for their own aggrandisement.

Shivaji's *ryots* experienced a new social order. This was not at all happening anywhere else. They could feel the difference. Their way of looking at their king and his work changed. They made both the king and his mission their own.

Shivaji and his Ryots

THE KING WITH AFFECTION FOR HIS RYOTS

Shivaji's father — Shahaji — was the chieftain of the Pune province. Even when the son was a teenager, the father asked him to supervise the province, with the help of Dadoji Kondadeo.

The Pune province lay on the border between the Mughal Empire and the Adilshahi dominion (Bijapur district). This region suffered from constant invasions by these rulers against each other. Their armies burnt down towns and villages, making settlements desolate. The *Sabhasad Bakhar*, a well-known chronicle, contains a graphic description of these ghastly happenings. Jungles took over the deserted villages and hamlets. Foxes, wolves and other beasts roamed freely over them.

Shivaji and Dadoji took over the administration of the region in this context. Shivaji awarded the right to these villages to those people who took it upon themselves to settle them. He encouraged those who came forward to work the land by supplying them with seeds and implements. Shivaji also maintained low rates for rent and taxes on land that had newly been brought under cultivation. No longer were taxes set at the whims and fancies of the collectors. Shivaji's officials measured the land and fixed the rent based on these measurements. Shivaji strictly ordered the tax collectors to muster only as much tax as had been legally fixed. In times of drought, the taxes were exempt. How were the peasants to pay tax if there was no produce? Shivaji understood the plight of peasants and acted accordingly. He not only exempted them from paying taxes and rent, he actually gave them extra help and aid. His orders had to be implemented to the letter and to its spirit.

AND THESE LANDLORDS

The *Sabhasad Bakhar* offers the following description:

From ancient times there used to be various feudatories. Those included Deshmukh, Deshpande, Desai, Patil, Kulkarni, Khot [revenue farmer], Mirasdar [land owner] and other landlords. They were chiefs of *Mahals* and villages. It was their job and right to collect revenue from the *ryots*. The government officers themselves did not directly collect the revenue. The main responsibility of doing so lay with such landlords. As a result they lorded over the people in those villages. They extracted taxes as they fancied. If a village owed to government about two hundred or three hundred rupees as taxes, the landlords squeezed two thousand or three thousand. Thus they deceived both the government as well as people to satisfy their own greed. They lived in mansions and fortresses and became arrogant by amassing guns, swords and keeping a large number of soldiers. When the government officers heard of such illegal activities of these feudatories, the former demanded more money. However, many powerful Deshmukhs and landlords did not respect their authority. On occasions, they even picked quarrels and disputes. All this resulted in provinces after provinces being infested with unruly thugs and looters.

Into this context, Shivaji tried to control the collection of taxes from peasant. Now look at this:

The Mahalkari [revenue official] measured total land in the state and registered in his records the names of those who tilled it. He used a stick to measure the land. Its length was about five arms and five fists. An arm was considered to be fourteen *tasus* long and the stick's length was eighty-two *tasus*. Twenty sticks made a *bigha* and hundred and twenty *bighas* a *chawar*. The crop estimate was made by just looking at the standing crop. It was agreed that the cultivating farmer kept for himself the third portion of his total produce while he paid two portions to the government. This was to be paid to the government in either kind or cash. In critical times such as droughts the government gave liberal loans to farmers. They were supposed to repay this amount in installments over a period of four to five years. If any land were to be newly brought under cultivation and it were to be given to a new cultivator who did not own any cattle to work with, the government supplied everything to him: the cattle, seeds and even grains and money for his sustenance until he harvested the crops. This had to be paid back after about four years. By giving such rights to till the land almost all the arable land was brought under cultivation. The officers were strictly warned to collect tax from the *ryots* proportionate to their income, that no force should be exerted on them to pay the taxes.

Shivaji put down all the disorder let loose by the feudatories and landlords. He appointed officers for collection of taxes. He made sure that the erstwhile landlords and feudatories could not harm the *ryots* in any manner; that their incomes were fixed on the basis of what they used to earn in earlier regimes; and that they should not collect the taxes directly from the *ryots*. Now they could get their portion of the government revenue without any risk. Only they had to get it sanctioned from the government every year. This put a tight check on their willful and unruly behavior and set the *ryots* free of their clutches. The *ryots* became free and happy. Maharaj destroyed the mansions and fortresses of these village officers, Deshmukhs and Deshpandes, who had enslaved the *ryots* and issued an order that they should not ever more resort to such uncivilized ways and should live in as simple and unpretentious houses as the *ryots*.

Would the *ryots*, then, not be devoted to the king who cared so much for the peasants and their land? Would they not feel that Shivaji's work should not only continue but also grow? Would the peasant boy of tender age not risk his life to challenge Shivaji's enemies?

The way the *ryots* deal with a king depends on how the king deals with them. If the king truly cares for the *ryots*, then they in turn care ten times for their king. If the rulers treat the state as the people's property and not their private property, then the *ryots* accept that state as their own. And if the rulers treat people as insignificant, then they hold the state as though it were inherited from their forefathers. *Ryots* rise to dethrone such rulers. Such is the history of the world.

SHIVAJI AND PROTECTION OF WOMEN

Some of the facts in Shivaji's life are indisputable; and nobody doubts those. Yet one cannot say for sure that all have realized their significance. Shivaji's attitude to women is one such case.

Women, especially poor women, were sexually oppressed and exploited in feudal times. Shivaji's time could not be an exception to this. Let alone kings and the princes, even their chieftains, feudatories, Patils, Deshmukhs and landlords treated the daughters and daughters-in-law of the poor as objects for their pleasure. They were raped in broad daylight and there was no one to turn to for justice. Those who were supposed to do justice were themselves complicit. They bestowed titles of honour and status on the criminals.

In such times, Shivaji's attitude in this respect was radically and fundamentally different. The story of the Patil of the village Ranjha is well-chronicled. In broad daylight, the officer Patil of the village picked up a poor peasant's young daughter and raped her. Instead of living the rest of her life in humiliation, she chose to die. She committed suicide. The whole village cried mutely. Shivaji heard the news of this crime and tragedy. He had the Patil arrested and brought to Pune. The Patil's arms and legs were cut off — as per the decreed punishment. The sentence was not only pronounced; it was implemented without delay. The people of Maval province could not believe their eyes or ears. The *ryots* gave their heart to Shivaji — the king who did not hesitate to punish a Patil, a feudatory, for raping a poor peasant's daughter. It was no surprise that they got ready to sacrifice their own life for his cause. The cause was their own cause: protecting women from such atrocities.

Of course a king requires feudatories to support his rule. But it requires one to have a very strong commitment to the value of justice to punish erring lords. Shivaji possessed this in abundance and this is the reason why the ryots participated in *Shivakarya,* Shivaji's cause. In our times too, in villages and in towns, the daughters and daughters-in-law of the poor ryots are being raped. What do those who claim his legacy and shout slogans in his name do? Are the culprits identified and punished? Leave alone cutting off the limbs, do such cases reach doorstep of the courts? Is it not the fact that the culprit is freed as fast as possible, depending upon his stature and his wealth?

Shivaji's times are not our times, but nonetheless, in a democracy he is worth recalling for just this reason: he gave himself to the people. We must remember Shivaji in order to challenge those who invoke his name and yet cover up their sins against democracy.

The story of the Ranjha Patil is not an exception. There are many more.

General Sakuji Gaikwad laid siege to the Belawadi fort in 1678. The chief of the fort was a woman. Her name was Savitribai Desai. This woman warrior defended the fort for twenty-seven days. But finally Sakuji succeeded in conquering the fort and, inebriated with victory, he raped Savitribai. Shivaji heard this and was so angry that he punished Sakuji by blinding him and imprisoning him for the rest of his life. He did not pardon a rapist even though he was his own victorious General. He could do so because he sincerely believed, "a woman's modesty, whoever she may be, must be protected at any cost." This was the height of progressive thinking of his time.

The celebrated story of the Kalyan Subedar's daughter-in-law has inspired many a poem and song. This beautiful young Muslim woman was presented to Shivaji in his court as a gift by one of his victorious warriors. Shivaji looked at her and said, "If only my *mother* was so beautiful!" To utter such words — again limited by his day — one needs to have rich character and a healthy attitude to beauty. Can we imagine what would happen if such a woman had come in front of today's uncivilized so-called *Shivabhaktas?* The difference lies between the real Shivaji and false Shivabhaktas.

Shivaji warned his generals and soldiers that no women, whether Hindu or Muslim, should be harmed in battles. He saw to it that those orders were enforced.

It was a regular practice in those times to carry concubines, prostitutes and zanana while on military campaigns. Both Hindu and Muslim kings and generals did this. It was customary to abduct women belonging to the enemy state, molest them and finally convert them into concubines. Shivaji issued strict orders that no one would take such concubines or prostitutes or women servants with them on campaigns. No woman was to be made a concubine.

We have entered the twenty-first century. Maharashtra claims to be a progressive and just state. Even today women are being raped. Those who support the perpetrators of such atrocities claim Shivaji's legacy and shout loud slogans in his name. What if Shivaji himself were to appear today? What kind of treatment would he give to these Shivabhaktas?

SHIVAJI AND LANGUAGE OF ADMINISTRATION

It has been more than fifty years since linguistic states were introduced in India. Maharashtra too has been a Marathi linguistic state for more than fifty years now. And still administration in the state is conducted in English. Will the purpose for which the linguistic states were formed ever be served? We drove away the foreign ruler but have not been able to get rid of the burden of English from our back. The native Sahib continues to speak in English. Being able to speak in English has become a status symbol and those who cannot are considered to be vulgar and backward.

The language of administration in Shivaji's time was mainly Persian. No language is inherently good or bad. But people did not understand Persian. Naturally, the administration that is conducted in a language that people do not understand does not appeal to them. Shivaji noted that people did not understand what was taking place in administration. He very thoughtfully set upon the work of compiling a compendium of the language of administration. He changed the administrative language to Marathi. Now the *ryots* felt closeness to the administration. They started to feel that Shivaji's state was their own.

SHIVAJI AND RYOTS

We saw how Shivaji's attitude to the women belonging to the poor populace, the *ryots*, was different from that of his contemporaries. He had a similar attitude regarding the *ryots'* property.

Any goon, as a right, could loot the property of the *ryots*. It was accepted as a matter of routine. Battles were also a daily affair. Armies and cavalries roamed freely from one place to another on campaigns. What happened to the *ryots'* property when the soldiers camped in and around village? The cavalries would romp unrestrained through the standing crops. The crop the peasants had raised through hard toil over the year, watered by their sweat, and ready for harvesting would be razed to the ground. The *ryots'* own king's army did this; to whom could they turn for succour? Who was there to lend them a sympathetic ear? The peasant could do nothing but blame his own fate and stay at home helplessly.

The armies were permitted to do whatever they wanted, without fear. It was in such time that Shivaji commanded his armies not to touch any vegetables grown by farmers, and asked his soldiers to buy articles of daily needs by making payments. It had become customary to see the hooves of the military horses trampling on their crops. Just imagine what the peasants must have felt when they now saw Shivaji's army carefully skirting the standing crops? What must they have felt about the king who took so much care of their crops, about the armies so obediently carrying out his commands? Would they not take his cause to their own heart?

Others did not stop at damaging crops alone. They used force as a matter of habit. What happened when the armies and their chiefs camped near a village? The fodder for the horses was collected from the village. The Patil or Kulkarni, the village officers, marshaled the entire village for their service. At a time when this kind of conduct was routine for the armies and their chiefs, when the *ryots* were used to accepting whatever was forced upon them as preordained by their destiny, a great man appears and issues such extraordinary commands to his army: *Do not touch even one vegetable*!

The fodder required for the horses is to be purchased by making cash payment. *In no case is the army to cause any harm to the ryots*!

Shivaji did not stop at issuing these orders. He enforced

them strictly. Such extraordinary empathy for the *ryots* and for their toil earned for him their unparalleled loyalty. Of course we do not encounter such chieftains and their cavalries today. But there are new chieftains and their motorcades. The modern day "chieftains" do not go on any campaigns but they do go on "inspection" and camp at places with their subordinates and the motorcade. How do these modern armies help themselves? Does the person who supplies meat and chicken receive its price? Do the new chieftains pay the expenses from their own pockets or salaries? Do they make their purchases by "making cash payments?" What do they really do? They all take care to display Shivaji's photograph in their house and office. They hail Shivaji at every second breath. What have they learnt from Shivaji? Which is their Shivaji? Which is the real Shivaji? Shall we tell them of Shivaji's strict command about not touching even the stem of a vegetable? This King is seen taking extraordinary care not to cause any harm to common people in his mission of defending the *Swaraj*.

The ethics of Shivaji's times can be found recorded in the various commands issued by Ramchandrapant Amatya. These various commands not only show a subtlety of mind of Amatya, they also exemplify his affection for people.

Wood naturally was important for the navy. There were thick jungles, rich in timbre. And yet look at the following striking command:

The wood of mango and jackfruit trees can be of great use for the navy. But do not allow anyone to touch them. These trees do not grow in a couple of years. The *ryots* planted them and nursed them like their own offspring. Their grief will know no bounds (if these trees are cut). Even if a tree is found dying, it should be bought from its owner, that too after he is persuaded to part with it and he totally satisfied, cuts it with his own hands.

V.K. Rajwade has recorded, in his eighth volume, some of the words of Shivaji himself. When his cavalry was camping near Chiplun, Shivaji laid down some do's and don'ts for his officers:

People must have stored hay for use during the rains and it could be lying about. If anyone, ignoring this, lights a bonfire or smokes a chillum the hay may catch fire and cause great harm to everyone. The whole of cavalry could be destroyed and you shall be held responsible for the death of the horses.

Or read this:

You have been given money. Whatever is needed must be bought from the market by paying cash. If you do not do so and harm the people, they will feel that the Mughals were better.

We do not find among his contemporaries a king or a feudal lord who had such sympathy for his people. Shivaji's affection and sympathy for his people was of a different order and therefore their loyalty to him was in turn of a very high order.

When the armies treated their own people as if they were their slaves and concubines, when those armies looted and plundered the *ryot's* property and wealth, raped their daughters and daughters-in-law, Shivaji's army behaved in an impeccable manner. The army was transformed under Shivaji. How? What was the reason?

This is a very important question.

The answer to this question cannot be found in Shivaji's mere character. It will also be inadequate to say that his commands were instrumental in this change. For a proper answer to this question we need to understand the very structure and the purpose of the existence of his army.

PEASANT ARMY

Kings of Shivaji's time kept standing armies. Fighting was their occupation. They earned their living by fighting wars. They used to be busy, throughout the year, in wars. The soldiers, who are away from their homes and the land they could have tilled, are bound to develop a reckless attitude. They do not care for anything. Such soldiers tend to be irresponsible. Such salaried soldiers do not care for the people. Their attitude is not congenial to be caring for the *ryots* and their wealth.

Shivaji's army was not the army of such professional soldiers. Not that there was no standing army. But most of the soldiers were practising farmers; they actually cultivated land. They lived with their families. At the same time they were soldiers. Ritual calendars marked tours: on *Simollanghan* [crossing the border] — a day of the *Vijayadashmi* festival — they would leave their villages to participate in military campaigns and return on the day of *Akshayya Tritiya* to their land and life. Such soldiers, who have a living and close relation to the family and the land, develop an attitude that cares for the land and wealth of other farmers. They respect the latter's women and daughters. When they see crops in someone else's farm they are reminded of their own crops and fields. When they see strange women they remember their own mothers, wives and daughters. Then they do not use force; they do not rape; they do not burn houses and crops. A person having living relations with the land as a peasant does not turn into a looter.

The section of society, the class from which a soldier comes — it is very important.

There is another very important point.

The armies of other kings were the armies of the looters. Looting was their very purpose. Why did the other kings want kingdoms? If not for loot, then for what else? Would they not loot? Those who were used to wallow in luxury did so by looting the *ryots* with the help of the armies. Why would they care for morals? Would they protect the *ryots'* wealth? Looting was not the motive for which Shivaji founded his kingdom. Nor was it the purpose of his army. On the contrary, it was to stop this kind of loot, which had been going on for ages. The army that was founded to stop such loot, to end oppression could not have itself resorted to such dastardly acts. Those who stand up to thwart oppression do not become oppressors.

It does not mean that Shivaji's army did not loot anytime and anywhere. He looted in the enemy lands. The loot of Surat is well known. But what was looted was wealth and it was done as a necessity. It did not involve other atrocities, such as violence against women.

There is one more point. Other kings did not pay salaries to their soldiers. Instead, a part of the loot was given to them. Naturally, the soldiers tended to loot as much as possible. Shivaji abolished this practice of giving part of the loot to his soldiers. It was replaced by a new practice of depositing the looted things into the treasury and paying the wage for the soldiers' work. Obviously, there was no vested interest for the soldiers to loot any longer. The soldiers used to get their wages irrespective of the fact whether they got the loot or not, whether the loot was small or big. This resulted in soldiers giving up the habit of looting for private gain.

Shivaji's personal morality was impeccable. All his commands were very clear and purposeful. He severely punished those who transgressed these commands. He raised his army from the productive peasants. His soldiers had living relation with farming and physical labour. He paid them in cash. Finally, he had devoted his life to the cause of ending injustice and plunder. All this resulted in moulding the character of his army. For the *ryots* Shivaji's army was not a gang of looters; on the contrary, they were saviours who had taken the responsibility of protecting them. The army protected the *ryots* and the *ryots* in turn supported it.

The relations between the army and the *ryots* need to be based on unity for running the state for their welfare. The people should not fear their own army. One succeeds in one's cause only if the army and the *ryots* are supportive of each other. There are modern examples where the people and the army share such relationship. The experience of Vietnam is fresh in our mind.

PROTECTION TO TRADE AND INDUSTRY

All modern states adopt the policy of charging severe taxes on the goods imported from foreign states. This is a policy of protecting indigenous trade and industry. But it is surprising to see that Shivaji, in a feudal society, charged such a tax to encourage indigenous trade.

On 6th December 1671, Shivaji wrote a letter to Sarsubedar of Kudal, Narhari Anandrao. The king asked his functionary to be vigilant while charging the octroi tax on salt at Sangameshwar. He exhorted the officer to keep the octroi elevated; otherwise outsiders would monopolize the entire trade. Shivaji cautioned his Sarsubedar not to allow the indigenous trade to become unviable. Here is one of the aspects of his farsightedness. He tended to both trade and agriculture on behalf of the people.

The Dutch traded in Maharashtra during the reign of Shivaji. When they asked him for permission to trade, he obliged with some conditions. One of the conditions was paying octroi. Shivaji's order, issued on 24th August 1677, permitted the Dutch to trade, saying,

> The Dutch Company is being permitted to carry out its trade in the Jinji Province. The Dutch shall have to pay an octroi of 2.5 per cent on their goods at Kuddalore. If advance information on the imports and exports is supplied the officers will not open the parcels for inspection. The Hawaldar officers are prohibited from allowing the goods to enter unless the proper tax is paid.

PROHIBITION OF THE SLAVE TRADE

Shivaji's order of 1677 contained a vital clause, which has remained unnoticed thus far. It says,

> You were permitted without hindrance, in the Musalman rule, to purchase or sell men and women as slaves. But under my rule you are not allowed the trade of men and women as slaves. If you try to do so, my people will stop you. This clause is to be strictly followed.

At this time, Indian men and women were captured and forcibly taken as slaves to work as labourers in foreign countries. Shivaji prohibited this slave trade — since he was the king of the *ryots*. It was Shivaji's state policy to look after his *ryots* well in all possible ways.

Shivaji and Religion

SHIVAJI'S APPROACH

What was Shivaji's approach to religion in general? What was his actual practice in this respect? How did he treat both Hindu and Muslim religions? These are historically very important questions. These are also relevant in today's times.

Shivaji was a Hindu. He was born in Maharashtra and it remained his place of operations throughout. Hindus therefore are proud of him. It is quite natural. Maharashtrian Hindus in particular are more proud of him. It is also very natural — nothing wrong in it. It is but human to look at one's own greatness, the greatness of one's own religion, and the greatness of one's own country or region in the light of the great heroes belonging to one's own religion. Moreover, the fewer the number of such heroic people in a community or a religion the more ordinary people take pride in them.

However, we tend to create, unconsciously, a larger than life image of such "heroes." Many times the image is deliberately projected as one-dimensional as it suits one's present day purposes and conveniences. In the process, a distortion creeps in and the image itself becomes distorted. It loses its identity.

There are several reasons why Shivaji's work, his administration, his time, his social reforms and his attitude to religion are not projected adhering to the historical truth.

His image in popular imagination is sometimes contrary to the truth.

Even an illiterate Maharashtrian knows Shivaji. They know the stories of his life. They know many things — places, names, incidences related to him. How did all this information reach out to the four corners of Maharashtra?

Innumerable ballads on Shivaji, his times, on miraculous, dramatic and sublime incidences in his life have been sung. Can one name a Marathi *shahir*, a bard, whether in Shivaji's time or even today, who has not sung of Shivaji? The answer is an emphatic "No." Every *shahir* has done it, and they are right to do so. The same is true of folk songs and all folklore. *Kirtanas* are no exception. Take anything — speeches, discourses, theatre and cinema. These are the means by which history is taken to people.

Distortions, interpolations in the historical accounts in the process of imaginative reconstruction, are not unlikely. Even if we overlook such distortions, we have to admit that the media mentioned above have their own natural limitations.

How can the miracles be done away with if the audience gathers to be entertained? The ballad would be quite uninteresting without some "imaginative" stories. Various figures of speech become indispensable, especially the hyperbole. If these "performances" were to only enumerate the figures of historical dates, and not use the figures of speech, if they were to logically analyze, and not to resort to the hyperbole, would there be a second "performance"? Moreover, the authors-performers have to take into account the level of understanding of their audiences. They themselves have their own limitations. All this has contributed to creating the image of Shivaji in the way we have received it. Of course there are many other factors involved in the distortion: self-interest, contemporary political expediency, a wrong approach to history or, at the least, inadequate understanding, and so on.

SHIVAJI AND MUSLIMS

Shivajis image, widespread amongst the masses, could be summarized thus: "Shivaji was anti-Muslim. His life mission was to oppose the Muslim religion. He was a protector of the Hindu religion. He was a Hindu Emperor (*Hindu Padpatshah*). He was a protector of cows and Brahmans (*Go-Brahman Pratipalaka*)."

A couplet by his contemporary poet, Bhushan, reflects this image. He wrote, "*Shivaji na hota, to sunta hoti sabki*" ("But for Shivaji, all would have been forcibly circumcised"). There have been such similar instances of misinterpretation held in a large number. "Shivaji's war was a kind of crusade. Religion was the inspiration of his mission, Shivaji fought for religion. He succeeded because he fought for religion. In fact, he was a reincarnation of God himself! He was the reincarnation of Vishnu or Shiva. God took on this reincarnation to save the religion. Goddess Bhavani gifted the sword to save the religion."

So on and so forth.

All these theories need to be tested against the historical facts. It will not be proper to uncritically accept them because we are Hindus or because they are convenient to us in the present circumstances. At the same time we should also beware of its flipside. There is a growing tendency among the Muslims to say, "We belong to the Muslim religion. It is our need to teach Muslims to hate Hindus. As many Hindus worship Shivaji; we should hold him as the savior of Hindu religion and as an aggressor of Muslim religion." Such an uncritical approach too is erroneous. What is the truth?

SHIVAJI, RANA PRATAP, PRITHVIRAJ CHAUHAN

Let us take the claim: Shivaji succeeded because he was a savior of Hindu religion. If this were the fact why did Rana Pratap or Prithviraj Chauhan not succeed? In actual fact, both of them were high caste Kshatriya Hindus. At least some people had doubts about Shivaji's being a Kshatriya. Both Rana Pratap and Prithviraj Chauhan were no less than Shivaji in respect of bravery, sacrifice, determination and hard work. Possibly they could be a grade better than him in these aspects. Then why did history take the course it did? If it was a religious crusade, why did one succeed and why were the other two badly defeated? If it was God's will that the Hindu Rashtra be founded then why was it founded in Maharashtra alone? Why did God not will that it be founded in Rana Pratap's and Prithviraj Chauhan's land as well?

It is not true that Shivaji succeeded because he believed in the Hindu religion. Evidence suggests that he set out to do something better for the world than merely save his religion.

Let us assume for a moment that his contemporary rulers belonged to a religion other than Islam. Suppose, there were kings belonging to the Hindu religion. Would Shivaji, then, hate Muslims? Why did Shivaji fight against the Muslim kings? Was it because they were Muslims or because they were kings? If he fought for both the reasons, then which of the two was the main reason? What was important: their being kings or their being Muslims?

RELIGIOUS TOLERANCE OF SOME MUSLIM KINGS

The historical record shows that not all Muslim kings were intolerant to Hindus and to the Hindu religion. History provides us with several instances of the tolerance of Muslim rulers. In Maharashtra, Shivaji's province, we find many Muslim rulers who had political and familial relations with Hindus. Dattatray Balwant Parasnis' *Marathe Sardar* offers the following analysis:

Marathas were very powerful in Nizam Shahi, Qutb Shahi and Adil Shahi. Gangavi, the founder of Nizam Shahi, who was converted to Islam, was the son of Bahirambhat Kulkarni, a Brahman. The father of Ahmednagar King too was a Hindu. Yusuf Adil Shah of Vijapur had married a Maratha girl. Qasim Barid was the founder of the throne of Bidar kingdom. His son also had married Sabaji's daughter. Owing to such relations and customs there was tolerance to Hindus and the Marathas were quite powerful in these kingdoms.

In the same book, Parasnis quotes Justice Mahadev Govind Ranade:

Hindus under the Southern Muslim kingdoms were encouraged by the kings (in many ways) and they were given many concessions and powers. This was because of a number of factors: alienation of the South Indian Muslims from the radical Muslims of the North, dominant position and a general goodwill of the Hindus in the Bahmani sultanate, the entry of Brahmans and Prabhus in the departments of Treasury and Tax Collection, entry of Marathi language in the administration because of them, the balance of forces resulting in Marathi warriors and officers getting promotions, the king's court donning a deep imprint as a consequence of his marriage with Hindu girls, and deep affection of those converted to Islam for the people of their own caste.

What does the name Hasan Gangu Bahmani, the founder of the Bahmani sultanate, tell us? A Muslim person called Hasan Jaffer had been working for a Brahman called Gangu. Later on he became a courtier of Tughlaq, the Emperor of Delhi. Gangu became the Emperor's *subedar* in Maharashtra. He rebelled against the Emperor and founded his own throne in Maharashtra. As a sign of gratitude to and in memory of his former master he adopted a new name, half Hindu and half Muslim: Hasan Gangu. His own state was called Bahmani, i.e., related to Brahmans. If the relations between the Hindus and the Muslims had always been of extreme enmity, this would not have happened.

Hindu lords and Hindus remained loyal to Muslim kings, and the latter were tolerant to their subjects. If the subjects — whether Hindus or Muslims — threatened the state and if the state became endangered, the kings would become intolerant. What was important was not their being Hindus or Muslims, but the stability of the state.

All the emperors of Delhi were not fundamentalist Muslims. This is an error of historical judgment. Akbar's tolerance is well-known. He even tried to found a new syncretic religion called Din-e-Ilahi. In his times there was considerable cultural unity. Hindu Todar Mal, as revenue Minister, used his intelligence for the cause of a king who happened to be a Muslim. Jagannath Pandit, a high caste Brahman, was happily writing Sanskrit poetry in the court of Shah Jahan.

A story of Pandit Jagannath is quite well known. The Hindu king of Jaipur made great efforts to get this Hindu Pandit under his tutelage so as to add to the king's status. Jagannath Pandit's reply to his invitation is very revealing,

> Only the Lord of Delhi or the Lord of the World has the might to fulfill my wishes. If any other king desires to do something for me it will be just enough for my hand to mouth existence.

The caste of the Lord of Delhi was not important. What was important was what he gave and how much he gave. Shah Jahan's son Dara Shikoh was a Sanskrit scholar. He used to regularly meet with the scholars from Kashi. In this milieu, someone composed the *Allopanishad* — or the Allah Upanishad — on the lines of the well-known Upanishads such as the Chandogya Upanishad and Brihadaranyaka Upanishad. It was a sign of cultural complexity.

A scholar of the stature of Tryambak Shankar Shejwalkar argued that if Dara Shikoh, Aurangzeb's elder brother, had ascended the throne rather than Aurangzeb, this continent would have come under one rule and would have become a very powerful country. In short, it can easily be seen that all the Muslim rulers were not the haters of the Hindus.

SHIVAJI'S MUSLIM LIEUTENANTS

Shivaji had many Muslims working under him. They held very important positions in his army and administration. Many of them were appointed to very high and responsible posts.

Those who study the life and work of Shivaji cite the formation of his navy as an example of his foresight. The Konkan coastline is very long, and a well-equipped navy was essential for its defense. Shivaji installed such a naval force, with its leader being Darya Sarang Daulat Khan. He was a Muslim.

Shivaji's personal bodyguard included a Muslim youth called Madari Mehtar. He was a trusted servant. Why should he, a Muslim, have helped Shivaji in his most dramatic and legendary escape from Agra? Would it have been possible if Shivaji had been a hater of Muslims?

Shivaji had many such Muslims in his employ. One of them was Kazi Hyder. After the battle of Saleri, Aurangzeb's lieutenants in the South sent a Hindu Brahman ambassador so as to establish amicable relations with Shivaji. Shivaji in turn sent Kazi Hyder as his emissary. Thus a Muslim ruler had under him a Hindu ambassador and a Hindu ruler had a Muslim. If society were vertically split between the Hindu and Muslim communities this could not have happened.

Siddi Hilal was one such Muslim working for Shivaji. Shivaji defeated Rustum Zama and Fazal Khan near Raibaug in 1660. Siddi Hilal fought on Shivaji's side. Adil Shah II's uncle Siddi Jauhar came to lay siege against Shivaji at Panhala Fort that same year. Shivaji's trusted aide, Netaji Palkar, used his armed detachments to dislodge the siege. Siddi Hilal and his son were at Netaji's side at the time. Hilal's son Siddi Wahwah was wounded and captured in this battle.

The Muslim chieftain Siddi Hilal, along with his son, fought for Shivaji, a Hindu, against a Muslim. Would this happen if the nature of wars at that time was communal, as a war between Hindus and Muslims? The chronicle *Sabhasad Bakhar* mentions the name of Shivaji's lieutenant — Shama Khan. V.K. Rajwade points out in his *Marathyanchya Itihasachi Sadhane* ("Sources of Maratha History") that Shivaji's Sarnobat or chief of infantry was Noor Khan Beg. These were not isolated individuals. Muslim sardars worked for Shivaji along with the anonymous Muslim soldiers under them.

Evidence of Shivaji's tolerance toward Muslims is found across the archives, deep in the chronicles of the time. Here is one example. Around 1648, about five hundred to seven hundred Pathans belonging to Vijapur army came to join Shivaji. Shivaji accepted the advice given to him at that time by Gomaji Naik Pansambal, his military advisor. Gomaji said, "These people have come hearing about your reputation. It will not be proper to turn them away. If you think that you should organize Hindus alone and will not be bothered about others, you will not succeed in establishing your rule. The one who wishes to establish rule must gather all the eighteen castes and the four *varnas* and assign to them their functions." Shivaji had not yet established his ecumenical policy in 1648. He would base his policy on such advice. Grant Duff, in his *History of the Marhattas* (1830) mentions Gomaji Naik's advice to Shivaji and then notes, "After this, Shivaji enlisted a large number of Muslims also in his army and this helped a great deal in founding his rule."

Shivaji's lieutenants, soldiers and chieftains were not Hindus alone. They were Muslims as well. If Shivaji had undertaken the task of eliminating Islam, these Muslims would certainly not have joined him. Shivaji had set out to demolish the *despotic and exploitative rule* of Muslim rulers. He had set out to bring in a rule that cared for the *ryots*. This is the reason why the Muslims too joined him in his cause.

The question of religion was not the main question. The main question was of the *state*.

Not loyalty to religion, but loyalty to the *state*, to a master was more important.

HINDU SARDARS UNDER MUSLIM RULERS

Just as there were Muslim Sardars and soldiers working with Shivaji, there were numerous Hindu Sardars and soldiers serving Muslim kings and emperors.

In fact Shivaji's own father, Shahaji, was an influential Sardar working for Adil Shah, Vijapur's Muslim ruler. Shahaji's father-in-law, Lakhuji Jadhav, was the Nizam's Mansabdar in Maharashtra. Adil Shahi's other Mansabdars included More of Javali, Nimbalkar of Phaltan, Khem Sawant of Sawantwadi and Suryarao Shringarpure of Shringarpur.

Mirza Raja Jai Singh, a high caste Rajput Hindu, came on behalf of the Mughal emperor to defeat Shivaji, force him to sign a humiliating agreement, took him to Agra, where he arrested him and his son Sambhaji. All he was doing was to serve honourably under a Mughal emperor. When Mirza Raja Jai Singh invaded Shivaji's dominion he had several Hindu Sardars under him. They were Jats, Marathas, Rajputs including Raja Rai Singh Sisodiya, Sujan Singh Bundela, Hari

Bhan Gaur, Uday Bhan Gaur, Sher Singh Rathod, Chaturbhuj Chauhan, Mitra Sen, Indra Man Bundela, Baji Chandrarao, Govind Rao, etc.

Tanaji Malusare, a lieutenant of Shivaji, died in action while capturing Fort Kondana. This fort was renamed as Simhagadh to commemorate Tanaji's heroic sacrifice. The officer in charge of Fort Kondana was a Hindu Rajput, Uday Bhanu, and he was a lieutenant of a Muslim Emperor.

There were about 500 Sardars holding different mansabs under Akbar. Out of those 22.5 per cent were Hindus. In Shah Jahan's empire, the ratio stood at 22.4 per cent. Aurangzeb is supposed to be the most fanatic of all the Muslim rulers. When he took over the empire, Hindus accounted for 21.6 per cent of the Mansabdars. When his reign ended, this figure rose to 31.6 per cent. It was Aurangzeb who had appointed Raja Jaswant Singh, a Hindu Rajput, as the Subedar (governor) of the Deccan. Aurangzeb's first Minister too was a Hindu, Raghunath Das. He was a Rajput and yet fought against Rajputs on behalf of Aurangzeb. One of Rana Pratap Singh's generals was Hakim Khan Soor, a Muslim. The Chief of the Peshwa's artillery in the battle of Panipat was Ibrahim Khan Gardi.

The Hindus who served Muslim Kings with loyalty and occasionally fought against them were not castigated as sinners or religious renegades. They were not called anti-Hindu or pro-Muslim. Loyalty to the Master, rather than to religion, was more important in those times.

In ancient or medieval India wars were not waged on the grounds of religion. The main motive behind wars was to capture or to strengthen power. It was true that religion was temporarily used to support the main purpose. But it never was the sole or main motive.

It is true that there were several Muslims working under Shivaji and many more working under Muslim rulers. Similarly it is revealing to see who fought against whom. It becomes very clear that these wars were not Hindus versus Muslims as such. Muslim rulers fought amongst themselves.

Babar, a Muslim, became the Emperor of Delhi by defeating Sultan Ibrahim Khan Lodhi, a Muslim. Babar founded the Mughal dynasty. Both Sher Shah and Humayun were Muslims yet they fought a bitter war against each other. The rulers of Bijapur and Golconda were both Muslims. Aurangzeb fought a protracted war against these so-called Muslim rules. This shows that what was important was not religion but power. If at all religion had any importance it was secondary. The primary concern was political power.

The legendary battle of Haldi was fought between Rana Pratap and Akbar. This battle had a great importance for Rana Pratap in particular, and for Rajputs and Rajasthan in general. But can this battle of Haldi be described, by any stretch of imagination, as a battle between Hindus and Muslims?

Akbar's army was led by the Rajput Man Singh. That army consisted of 60,000 Mughal troops and 40,000 Rajput troops. Whereas Rana Pratap's army had 40,000 Rajput soldiers, it consisted of a large division of Pathans under Hakim Khan Soor. It also had a cavalry under a Pathan called Taj Khan. The chief of Rana Pratap's artillery too was a Muslim Sardar.

Guru Govind Singh too fought against the central Muslim power. His army also had, along with Sikhs, thousands of

Muslims. After Aurangzeb died, there was a fierce struggle for succession among his heirs. Guru Govind Singh helped Bahadur Shah in that feud.

The religious basis behind the uprising by the Jats, Rajputs, Marathas and Sikhs was flimsy. Their uprisings were basically against despotic central rule. The soldiers and noblemen were loyal to their masters irrespective of religion. Neither Hindu nationalism nor the mission of spreading Islam inspired the standing armies of the feudal period. To serve a master as long as he fed, was the general social practice.

LOOT AND DESTRUCTION OF TEMPLES

The refrain of fundamentalist Hindu organisations is commonly heard: "The Muslim kings were cruel and barbaric. They destroyed and desecrated temples. They attacked the Hindu religion. Therefore, all the Muslims are necessarily anti-Hindu. And, since they are anti-Hindu, the Hindus also must have to be anti-Muslim."

Just as Hindu organisations use this kind of argument, the Muslim organisations too use a similar argument.

They tell their followers, "Hindu religion is the religion of *Kafirs*. What our forefathers did to destroy it was quite correct. If possible, we should also do the same. We should be at least against the Hindus." The organisations tell their followers to regret the loss of their rule. They use such language to organise themselves on a religious basis.

It is true that the invading Muslim armies, while expanding their rule, looted and destroyed temples. But this is not the whole truth. It is a half-truth. The tribe-like armies of Arabs, Turks and Afghans were not regularly paid. It was an accepted practice for them to loot and keep their share with them as wage. Certain Hindu temples used to be very rich. While looting, the invaders destroyed some temples and divided the booty.

These armies would not care to touch the temples situated atop mountain peaks or deep inside the ravines. What could be the reason for this? The main purpose was to loot the wealth in temples and not to destroy them.

Looting wealth was the prime concern; religion was secondary. Destruction of temples was a means of achieving this purpose. A major portion of this loot went to the king. It was the chief source of the king's revenue.

A second motive of attacking temples was to discourage the people who live in areas surrounding the temples. The violence was intended to create fear among them, to break their fighting spirit. People believed in religion and in god. It was easy for the invaders to make them believe that those who had looted god would easily loot them too. "Such a powerful god could not do anything; what can we mortals do?" This kind of helplessness and panic would spread all over. This would make it easy for the invaders to conquer the enemy. In Shivaji's time, temples were not centers of religion alone. They were centers of wealth, of power and status. There was another benefit of looting temples. The invaders claimed that they were breaking the temples of *kafirs*, that they were destroying their religion. This worked as a camouflage to hide the real thing, the loot of wealth. This would help in garnering support of the priestly elites, *mullahs* and *maulavis*, as a device to get the support of the Muslim masses. Religion was used as a ruse to cover foul deeds.

LOOT FOLLOWED BY ENDOWMENTS

The rulers who initially looted and demolished temples on their way to assuming power, would, once the enemy kingdom was conquered and their own rule was stabilized, award endowments and grants to those very temples. There are numerous such examples.

Aurangzeb, who is known as a religious fanatic, destroyed many temples while invading kingdoms to expand his own empire. But the same Aurangzeb donated money to temples. He awarded two hundred villages to the Jagannath temple of Ahmedabad. He donated money to Hindu temples at Mathura and Benaras too.

There are differences among scholars as to whether the Adil Shahi commander and Shivaji's adversary, Afzal Khan, broke the idols in Pandharpur and Tuljapur temples. Some believe he did. Tryambak Shankar Shejwalkar, however, suggests otherwise. He writes that the idols in place today in these temples are quite ancient. Whatever the truth, it is recorded in the chronicles that Afzal Khan, while camping at Wai before launching his assault on Shivaji at Pratapgadh, not only continued the traditional rights of Brahman priests but also awarded new ones. Moreover, can we forget that when Afzal Khan supposedly destroyed the Bhavani temple at Tuljapur, he was accompanied by Pilaji Mohite, Shankarraoji Mohite, Kalyanrao Yadav, Naikji Sarate, Nagoji Pandhare, Prataprao More, Zunjarrao Ghatge, Kate, Baji Ghorpade and Sambhajirao Bhonsle. It is well known that Goddess Sharada temple at Shringeri was damaged while the Marathas looted it in 1791 and the Muslim King Tipu Sultan restored it later.

Why was money donated to temples after a rule was stabilized? It was done to appease the sentiments of the Hindus and prevent any rebellion against the new rulers. Because of this, the Muslim rulers encouraged such donations.

Political power was the cause for looting and demolishing temples. It was the motivation of political power, once more, that led to the donations of money and property toward the repair of destroyed temples and the construction of new ones.

DOMINANCE OF POWER, SUBORDINATION OF RELIGION

Muslim kings were not alone in their loot of temples. Hindu kings also looted temples for their wealth.

Chronicles such as Kalhana's *Rajatarangini* tell us that Harsha Dev, king of Kashmir, used to loot Hindu temples. He would melt idols for their metals. Harsha would even desecrate the idols by sprinkling them with human waste and urine before melting. What we do not find in these chronicles is evidence of communal riots having taken place because of the desecration of these idols by Harsha. It is telling that the revenue department of Harsha's administration had a section called *Devotpatan*, Demolition of Gods.

If the Muslims started being a hindrance and a nuisance to the Muslim rule, the rulers would not hesitate to harass them in spite of the Mullahs and Maulavis. Marathi *bakhars* accuse Mohammed bin Tughlaq of massacring Mullahs and Sayyeds. Some historical accounts describe the fear amongst Mullahs of Emperor Jahangir. When he approached, some would hide.

What is the conclusion of all this? More important for the rulers of that era was their power, not their religion.

SHIVAJI'S WARS AGAINST MARATHAS AND HINDUS

Shivaji fought several big and small wars to found his kingdom. The rulers before him in the area were mainly Muslims. He waged wars against them. At the same time, Shivaji had to fight the Marathas as well. His was not a war against Islam, but a war for power. In *Marathi Riyasat*, Riyasatkar Sardesai writes, "The war against Vijapurkars did not mean the war between Hindus and Muslims. It could not have acquired such character." There are meticulously kept historical records about this. It is not right to ignore them.

Shivaji faced an enormous challenge from powerful Maratha noblemen who served the Vijapurkars, such as Mohite, Ghorpade, More, Sawant, Dalavi, Surve, and Nimbalkar. Riyasatkar Sardesai, Krisnajee Anant Sabhasad (who wrote a *bakhar* for Shivaji), Grant Duff and Parasnis list the names of great and powerful Maratha noblemen who opposed Shivaji. They did not respect Shivaji and challenged his authority. Why were these and other such Hindu-Maratha noblemen against Shivaji? They were all Hindus. They observed their religion with great faith. If Shivaji had undertaken the cause of protecting the Hindu religion — a *Dharmakarya* — why should all these Hindu noblemen have opposed him? Sardesai writes, "They feared to lose what they possessed." What did they possess? Grant Duff describes Shivaji as a destroyer. What did he destroy? "In the regions that he won from the Vijapurkars, Shivaji replaced the old system of monopoly in tax collection with the collection of revenue based on evaluation of yields of crops every year." This makes Shivaji's destruction clear. Duff was angry that Shivaji had destroyed the monopoly system. But Capon's ethical judgment could not help itself, "It was possibly beneficial to the people." It was obvious who benefitted from Shivaji and who was disenfranchised.

The chief Maratha Hindu noblemen (Ghatge, Khandagale, Baji Ghorpade, Baji Mohite, Nimbalkar, Dabir, More, Bandal Sawant, Surve, Khopade, Pandhare, the Desais of Konkan and the Deshmukhs of Maval) all opposed Shivaji because of their vested interests. Shivaji's close relations — Vyankoji Bhonsle and Mambaji Bhonsle as well as Jagdevrao Jadhav and Rathoji Mane — stood against him. It is no surprise that when Shaista Khan invaded Shivaji's dominion from the north, Hindu noblemen accompanied him. Among the Maratha noblemen who joined Shaista Khan, we number Sakhaji Gaikwad, Dinkarrao Kakade, Rambhajirao Pawar, Sarjerao Ghatge, Kamlojirao Kakade, Jaswantrao Kakade. Tryambkrao Khandagale, Kanakojirao Gade, Antajirao and Dattajirao Khandagale. More surprising and painful is the fact that Shivaji's own blood relations, Tryambakraoji, Jivajirao, Balajiraje and Parasojiraje Bhonsle were with the Mughal warlord, Shaista Khan. This Mughal army included Dattajiraje and Rustumrao Jadhav of Sindkhed. These Jadhavs were from Jijabai's family. Krishnaji Kalbhor of Loni had joined Shaista Khan with the hope of obtaining the fiefdom of Pune. Shaista Khan confiscated the Deshmukhi from Shitole and awarded it to Kalbhor. Balajirao Honap lived near Lal Mahal in Pune. He had spent some time of his life under the protection of the umbrella of the *Swaraj*. But he felt more affinity to Shaista Khan than to Shivaji. Such were the Hindus. So much for their religiously-defined identity! Their loyalty was to their fief. It is clear as daylight. The only exception was Kanhoji Jedhe.

Shivaji held a very clear, and very bitter, view of these lords and noblemen. His Prime Minister has said, "They have a natural predisposition, a natural hunger to become powerful, to rob others. They become friendly with the enemy on the eve of the latter's invasion with the hope of obtaining a fief. They meet the enemy on their own, without invitation. They pass on the secret information and abet the enemy's entry into our state. They kill the nation." The fief was all. Their religion was marginal. They burned for their fief, not for their religion.

SHIVAJI'S FAITH

Shivaji was not a non-believer or an atheist. He did not declare his state to be secular. Shivaji was a Hindu. He had faith in religion. He worshipped gods, goddesses and saints as well as donated wealth to temples.

But was he against Islam? If he had faith in his religion, did it mean that he hated Islam? Was it his intention or effort to Hinduise the Muslims? Was he trying to *Maharashtrianise* them?

If we wish to be faithful to history, the answers to these questions are plainly negative.

Shivaji had looted Surat on two occasions. The detailed accounts of both are well recorded. There are also records of the looting of the market at Junnar and other places. However, is there the tiniest of evidence that he demolished a single mosque? Or is there any evidence of him having constructed a temple in place of a mosque, which was supposed to have been built by demolishing a temple? Not at all. On the contrary, there are records that he donated money and land to mosques. Sabhasad's *Bakhar* notes, "There were places of worship all over. Proper arrangement of their worship and care was made. He also looked after the arrangements in pirs and mosques."

What was true of the mosques was also true of the Muslim sadhus and saints. Shivaji and his contemporary Marathas and Hindus worshipped and donated money to *dargahs*. They respected Muslim sadhus, pirs and fakirs. Shivaji had many gurus. They included a Muslim saint called Yakut Baba.

Shivaji's tolerance for Muslim religion is recorded in many ways in historical documents. Khafi Khan's *Muntakhabu-l Lubab* notes, "Shivaji had made a strict rule that wherever his soldiers went they were not to harm mosques, the Quran or women. If he found a volume of Quran, he would show respect to it and hand it over to his Muslim servant. If any helpless Hindu or Muslim were found, Shivaji would personally look after them until their relatives came to take them." Shivaji's chief justice, Raghunath Pandit Rao, in a letter of 2nd November 1669 writes, "Shrimant Mararaj has ordained that everybody is free to follow his religion and nobody is allowed to disturb it."

Those who try to appropriate Shivaji for their narrow purposes will have to answer for the historical record. If there are any buyers for their hatred for Islam they should sell it on their own merit. They should not sell their commodity in Shivaji's name. They should not sell that commodity under the brand of Shivaji.

At the same time, Muslims should not equate Shivaji with his image created by these so-called Shivabhaktas. They should look at history; they should appreciate his attitude to Islam. Only then should they form their opinion.

Shivaji was Hindu and he believed in his religion. But, as the king, he did not discriminate against his people on the basis of religion. He did not treat Hindus in one way and Muslims in another. He did not discriminate against Muslims because they belonged to another religion. Both Hindus and Muslims must understand this.

There were two kinds of Islamic kings. Some, like Akbar, were tolerant to Hindus. Some, like Aurangzeb, were intolerant. Aurangzeb levied the *jaziya* tax at the behest of the mullahs and the maulvis. There was an uprising against this tax. Shivaji wrote a letter, in Persian, to Aurangzeb about this. The letter gives a graphic idea of how Shivaji looked at various religions. Shivaji writes that levying the *jaziya* tax on the poor and helpless populace is against the basic tenets of Mughal rule. Aurangzeb's great-grandfather Akbar had ruled for fifty-two years. He treated everyone with justice. The people therefore honored him as Jagatguru. Jahangir and Shah Jahan continued his policy. All of them became famous all over the world for this. These emperors could easily have collected the *jaziya* tax, but they did not do so. That is why they could become so rich and so honoured. Their empires grew. But in Aurangzeb's rule both Hindu and Muslim soldiers were unhappy. The price of grains went up. It was not reasonable, as far as Shivaji was concerned, for the empire to collect the *jaziya* tax from poor Brahmans, Jogis, Bairagis, Jain Sadhus and Sanyasis. Such an act would ultimately only discredit the Mughal dynasty. Shivaji writes, "The Quran is the word of God himself. It is a heavenly Book. It calls God the "God of the entire World." It does not call him the God of Muslims alone. This is because both Hindus and Muslims are one before him. When the Muslims pray in the mosques, they in fact pray to *Bhagwan*. And Hindus too do the same when they toll the bell in a temple. To oppress a religion is therefore to pronounce enmity with God."

Shivaji therefore appeals to Aurangzeb not to ignore reason. The Sultan of Gujarat had earlier sacrificed reason. But he had to pay for it. The Emperor would have to pay similarly. "Any inflammable matter burns out if it comes in contact with fire. Similarly, any rule perishes in people's discontent. The fire of rebellion, born of the torture of innocents, can burn the whole kingdom faster than any fire. The Emperor therefore should not discriminate against any religious creed and oppress them. People, like insects, are harmless. However, if Hindu people are subjected to misery, your empire will be reduced to ashes in the fire of their anger."

Shivaji has propounded an important principle for us Indians here. Akbar and other emperors did not subject the Indian people to religious cruelty and oppression. Because of such religious tolerance Akbar was hailed as Jagatguru. But Aurangzeb, by taxing poor people, acted against the principles of Islam. If the Quran is the word of God, for God Hindus and Muslims are not different. If the king harms people, they will destroy him, however powerful he might be.

In the context of his time, Shivaji's thoughts and his policy were unique and unparalleled. Religion had a deep impact upon people's life. But Shivaji taught us that other religions are as great as one's own religion, and that though the forms of worship in each religion are different their goal is one. The thoughts of Akbar, Dara Shikoh and Ibrahim Adil Shah were not different from this.

Shivaji was religious. He was proud of being a Hindu. He awarded large gifts to temples and Brahmans. All this is true. However, his pride in his religion was not based on the hatred for other religions. He never thought that he could not be a great Hindu unless he hated Muslims. Even in medieval times his faith in religion was rational.

Shivaji and Brahmans

Many titles are prefixed to Shivaji's name. *Go-Brahman Pratipalak* (Protector of cows and Brahmans) is the most well known. It is consistently propagated that he was a protector of cows and Brahmans.

Shivaji's many letters — all authenticated — are now available. In none of his letters has he claimed to be a *Go-Brahman Pratipalak*. Many of his contemporaries wrote to him, and none of them give him this prefix. There are twenty-nine letters that are from the period after he became king. In each of these letters he calls himself *Kshatriya Kulawatans Shri Raja Shiv Chhatrapati*. He does not call himself *Go-Brahman Pratipalak*. Then where does this *Go-Brahman Pratipalak* tradition come from?

B.M. Purandare, who has written widely on Shivaji, says that he called himself *Go-Brahman Pratipalak*. As evidence, Purandare cites *Shiv Charitra Sadhane* (vol. V, articles 534 and 537). The scholar T.S. Shejwalkar examines the evidence thoroughly and concludes that in article 534, Shivaji does not call himself *Go-Brahman Pratipalak*; indeed, it is a Brahman quoted in the letter who uses this phrase. In article 537, there is no mention of *Go-Brahman Pratipalak* all. The statement by Purandare is a white lie! There is a world of difference between Shivaji calling himself *Go-Brahman Pratipalak* and a Brahman who wrote him a letter doing so. Any one who has gone to a king asking for alms or, at any rate, asking for a favour would naturally call him a protector. What is so special about it?

Who might have appended this title to Shivaji? The cows could not possibly have done so. The answer, therefore, is more than clear. To attach titles to great historical figures as a matter of convenience is an act, at the most, of cleverness and cunning. Such acts go unnoticed as long as people do not go to the root of the matter. But this does not make such an act of cunning a historical truth.

Shivaji did prohibit his soldiers from theft of cows, *ryots* and women. This is mentioned in Grant Duff's book, *The History of the Mahrattas*. How did Shivaji, a *pratipalak* of cows, *ryots* and women become, out of the blue, the *Go-Brahman Pratipalak*? Who made him so? It should not be difficult to guess who substituted Brahmans in place of *ryots* and women.

Brahmans do not seem to have any privileges in Shivaji's kingdom. In a letter, Shivaji writes about a Brahman who had done some mischief and says that he should not be spared punishment because he is a Brahman. He says, "Those who behave as an enemy, will be treated as such." All Brahmans did not side with Shivaji. It is a good indicator of why he did not adopt the title, *Go-Brahman Pratipalak*. The chronicles bristle with amusing anecdotes to make this point. To oppose Shivaji, some Brahmans in his kingdom performed a *yajna* called Kot Chandi Yajna. They conducted this *yajna* on behalf of Mirza Raja Jai Singh, the mighty nobleman who served the Emperor of Delhi; they wished him victory. A chronicle describes the scene:

Mirza Raja was worried that Shivaji, very brave and clever, was fond of battle. He was a very skillful warrior. He had personally killed Afzal Khan. He ran riot in the camp of Shaista Khan. Mirza Raja was therefore worried about his own success. The great Brahman priests suggested a way. He would succeed if he performed a *yajna*. Then Mirza said, "Prepare a Kot Chandi and eleven crore *lingas*. Chanting should be practised to fulfill my desire." He thus arranged for four hundred Brahmans to sit for the *yajna*. The *yajna* and prayers continued round the clock. He set aside two crore rupees for the *yajna* and it went on for three months. After completion of the *yajna* the Brahmans were properly rewarded and then he set on his campaign.

If Shivaji was a *Go-Brahman Pratipalak* and his rule was for the protection of Brahmans and the Hindu religion, why did Brahmans perform such a massive Kot Chandi *yajna*?

BRAHMANS' OPPOSITION TO SHIVAJI'S
ANOINTMENT AS CHHATRAPATI

Many Brahmans of Maharashtra opposed the anointment of Shivaji as king. This is a well-known fact. According to the system of *Chaturvarna* and the old Hindu laws, only Brahmans and Kshatriyas had the right to become a king. Even though Shivaji was a warrior, even though he had conquered what could easily be a kingdom, religious law said that he was not entitled to be a king. Some doubted his being a Kshatriya. And others did not bother whether he was a Kshatriya or not. For them, even if he belonged to the Kshatriya *kula*, he did not remain a Kshatriya because he had suffered *samskar kshaya*. His *maunji bandhan* [thread ceremony] was not performed. His wedding was not performed according to proper rituals. How, then, could he be king?

Some very orthodox Brahmans went to the extreme. They said that the Kshatriyas no longer existed after the Nanda dynasty (*Nandantam Kshatriya Kulam*). In Akbar's time, Krishna Bhat Shesha wrote a treatise, *Shudrachar Shiromani*, in which he argued that Parashuram had wiped out the Kshatriyas from the face of the earth. No longer do Kshatriyas with kingly qualities and belonging to kingly dynasties exist. In this situation, how could Shivaji be anointed a king?

Not a single Brahman from Maharashtra was ready to perform the rituals associated with his anointment. Gaga Bhatta came from Benares to anoint Shivaji by performing the Vedic rituals. Gaga Bhatta's family had roots in Nanded (Maharashtra), but his reputation was built in Benares. Shivaji rewarded them with sumptuous gifts, so much gold that it was too heavy to carry down the Raigadh fort.

SHIVAJI'S BRAHMAN COMRADES

Brahmans from Maharashtra had opposed Shivaji's anointment. Some Brahmans even performed a *yajna* on behalf of Mirza Raja Jai Singh against Shivaji. Such evidence does not mean that all Brahmans from Maharashtra opposed Shivaji.

The question of Shivaji's caste and kingly virtues was not a personal one. It was not about this or that particular priest. What was raised by the Brahmans in their objection to Shivaji was the basic question of *Chaturvarna*, the system of caste. That question remains alive today.

The Dharma of the Brahmans ordains that Shudras

cannot be kings. This is because, as the legend suggests, Shudras are born of Prajapita's feet. It is therefore their religious duty to serve the three upper varnas. God partially exists in a king. It is impossible for God to be present in a Shudra. Thus this religious tradition insists that a Shudra can never become a king. A Muslim can be a king, but a Shudra cannot. This is what the orthodox Hindu religion says. It was religion *itself* that was opposed to Shivaji's anointment. It was not the opposition by all Brahmans as such.

In fact there were many Brahmans who lent their hand in constructing the Shivaji's *Swaraj*. Dadoji Kondadeo was in charge of the Pune region. Shivaji's cabinet held important Brahmans — Moropant Pingale (Peshwa), Anaji Datto and Dattaji Trimbak (the latter were also accomplished warriors). When Shivaji escaped from Agra, he was helped along by four Brahmans — Tryambakpant Dabir and Raghunathpant Korde from Maharashtra and Krishnaji Kashi and Visaji from North India.

The objection to Shivaji did not come from Brahmans as such. It came from the tenets of orthodox Hinduism. Shivaji had to accept the historical limitations, some of which pushed him to participate in ridiculous events. At the age of 44, Shivaji allowed Gaga Bhatta to perform his *maunji bandhan* to counter the objection that he had lost *samskaras*. He allowed himself to be remarried to the chants of the mantras, and to give away a large amount of gold. All of this to appease orthodox Hinduism so that he could be anointed as king.

Opportunist fundamentalists of today try to attach the title "The Protector of the Hindu Religion" to Shivaji. Can they hide the historical truth that the same Hindu religion and the Protectors of Religion amongst the Brahmans opposed Shivaji's anointment? That they made him get his *maunji bandhan* done at the age of forty-four and to re-marry his wife? How ridiculous!

Shivaji followed the tenets of his religion. He was limited by his times. Even great individuals are subject to the constraints of their historical time, the constraints of their circumstances.

Others tend to extol Shivaji's deeds in a ridiculous manner — saying his state was secular and that he was a socialist. Of course this is not true. Shivaji was a king in a feudal society and therefore he could not have been secular. It was impossible that he would be socialist. More important is his foresight, far superior to his contemporaries — which enabled him to enact many progressive measures. What is different is the way he showed compassion and affection for the *ryots*.

Shivaji was a product of his times, a believer in some of its sensibilities. Shivaji was crowned at Raigadh on 5th June 1674. But then he had a second coronation, three months after the first one. Why did he do this? After his first coronation, a series of deaths took place: Shivaji's mother, Jijabai, died on the thirteenth day after the coronation; his Chief of Army, Prataprao Gujar, died shortly afterwards; one of Shivaji's wives, Kashibai, died. A Yajurvedi Tantrik, Nishchalpuri Gosavi, came to see Shivaji. He told him that these tragedies took place because Gaga Bhatta had committed certain errors in the ceremonial rites for coronation, including holding the coronation on an inauspicious date. Since Gaga Bhatta did not offer animal sacrifice, certain deities remained dissatisfied. Shivaji was wary of the commission of "sins." He accepted

Nishchalpuri's arguments and had another coronation, with more *yajnas* and more gifts distributed to the Brahmans. In the historical record anywhere in the world, we have no evidence of another king being crowned twice! Double coronation and more gifts to deities and Brahmans did not help Shivaji. He survived a mere six years as king and died at a very young age. That Shivaji had two coronations shows us that he was a man of his times, and has to be seen as such — neither a Hindu fundamentalist nor a secular socialist.

96 GREAT FAMILIES OPPOSE SHIVAJI

Brahmans considered Shivaji to be a Shudra, a man of a low caste. Maratha noblemen who belonged to the 96 Great Families regarded themselves as Kshatriyas, and did not initially accept Shivaji as king. Even though these 96 had no kingdom, they called themselves kings (*Raja*) or *Patils*. They would attach the title Raja or Patil to their names, so that they become Shinde Raja, More Raja, Landage Patil, Kolhe Patil, Kale Patil, Vikhe Patil . . . . The habit of attaching Patil to the name is prominent in Ahmednagar district, where almost all Marathas add the title to their names.

Chandrarao More Raja of Jawali, a nobleman of the Shah of Bijapur, was one of the 96. Shivaji tried to enlist More for the cause of *Swaraj*. Letters and emissaries went to More, who did not respond to these genuine efforts. Shivaji then warned him: if Chandrarao did not join Shivaji, Jawali would be captured and More arrested. Shivaji had referred to himself in the letter as "King." More arrogantly replied, "You, a king? You become a king because you choose to call yourself one. If you are eating your meal, finish it and come to Jawali to wash your hands. Let's fight!" Shivaji fulfilled More's wish. He went to war and captured Jawali. The point to note is More's refusal to accept Shivaji's claim to kingship.

In short, whether high-caste Brahmans or high-caste Marathas, they were not initially prepared to accept Shivaji Bhonsle as their leader and King. Even today the Marathas who arrange marriages on the basis of caste-family status and traditions treat the persons having the surname Bhonsle as lowly.

Shivaji had to suffer the inequities imposed by the system of the four varnas. He found a way out within the given religious framework because he followed his religion. He got his anointment done as per the wishes and rights of Brahmans. He won his kingdom by his strength and bravery, as well as by clever strategies and tactics. Even Aurangzeb respected him. But the upholders of Hindu religion did not respect him. That is why he had to get his coronation performed twice. He had to obtain the consent of religious leaders.

KULWADI BHUSHAN

Mahatma Jotirao Phule wrote a ballad on Shivaji. Right at the beginning of this ballad Phule calls Shivaji "Kulwadi Bhushan" (Jewel in the Crown of Peasants). He concludes the ballad thus, "Jotirao Phule sings, son of Kshudra." In short, Shivaji Bhonsle was a son of the Shudras. He was a peasant. Mahatma Phule was not a researcher or a historian. He was an active social reformer committed to the cause of equality. One may argue therefore that Phule was biased in a particular way and there was no historical support to his claims. Historians are in disagreement over Phule's claim. They write tentatively and with great hesitation. But, at the least, they hold differing views.

Mahamahopadhyaya Datta Waman Potdar, an eminent scholar, has studied the evidence of Shivaji's family. He writes,

> It is very difficult to decide the lineage of the family. Many later documents, even some belonging to the period immediately prior to Shahu Maharaj, have recorded how enquiries were made from Udaipur as to whether most of the families belonged to Sisodias or not at all. There were differences about their previous lineage being of Sisodias. I personally do not doubt that Shivaji was a Rajput and his Bhonsle family was one of the Sisodias of Rajputana. In fact Shahaji in one of his letters makes it a point to say, "I'm a Rajput." This makes the matter more than clear.

Whether Shivaji was a Kshatriya by birth is a meaningless controversy. Some people may claim, implicitly or explicitly, their greatness through relations with Shivaji. "Shivaji was a Kshatriya — I'm a Kshatriya too." Or, "Shivaji's surname was Bhonsle. I'm also a Bhonsle." Let them indulge in their fantasy. Those who have nothing else, apart from the caste or family lineage, as a claim for greatness are free to discuss the lineage of Shivaji's family. Shivaji's achievements are of greater significance than his family's antecedents. We can hardly choose the family we are born in. But it is certainly in our hands to make of our life what we will — at least some of it! Of course, those who do not have any ability to do anything significant will only sing the paeans of lineage and racial superiority.

SHIVAJI'S PEASANT COMRADES

If anybody uses Shivaji's name to establish the superiority of the varnas, they will be judged false by the historical record. Who participated in Shivaji's historic mission? The majority of his colleagues in his Herculean task of creating *Swaraj* were not from the higher castes. Nor were they noblemen or landlords and other feudatories. They rose from the lowest strata of society. They came from the low castes. They were poor peasants. They were Shivaji's peasant comrades.

Shivaji's *mavlas*, his soldiers, were the backbone of his work. They faced their adversaries with great tenacity. Pure, unblemished loyalty and love linked them to Shivaji. His unparalleled acts of bravery could only be possible because of the boundless sacrifice of the *mavlas*, the peasant soldiers.

Established noblemen and feudal lords did not help Shivaji initially. Shivaji, therefore, created new generals and lieutenants from amongst the poor families. They became great by their bravery and their contribution to the making of *Swaraj*. Take the case of the barbers Shiva and Jiva Mahala. Shiva helped Shivaji escape from Panhala Fort. Jiva Mahala Sankpal from Mauje Kondivali (Jawali) was with Shivaji when he assassinated Afzal Khan. Shivaji's Chief of Intelligence was Bahirjee Naik (from the "untouchable" Ramoshi community). Shivaji took the peasants who lived on the fields to establish his kingdom.

Historical evidence shows us that such acts were not the domain only of individuals. Entire communities participated in Shivaji's historical undertaking. Shivaji employed people from the Berad, Ramoshi and Adekari communities according to their qualities and abilities, says the *Sabhasad*

SHIVAJI AND BRAHMANS

Bakhar. Crime declined in his reign, as those who had been branded as criminals got an opportunity to use their ability and bravery for good.

Shivaji's Naval Chief was a Muslim. Most of his sailors and soldiers came from the Koli, Sonkoli, Bhandari and Muslim communities. Shivaji transformed those who toiled on the sea into soldiers of the sea. Shivaji turned the commoners into great people. They, in turn, made him a great king. Both came together to fulfill a tremendous task.

A good idea, when common people accept it, becomes a force and such force allows common people to perform uncommon deeds. Extraordinary events in history do not take place unless the common people participate in them.

Those who belonged to the elite did not want to change the *status quo.* Those who belong to the poor desired change. Shivaji organised them, enlightened them, gave them status and put a halt to injustice. Those who suffer injustice come forward to destroy it. Those who perpetrate injustice do not end it.

SHIVAJI AND CONVERSIONS

Shivaji was a Hindu, but not an intolerant Hindu. On many occasions, Shivaji did things that were seen as unacceptable to religion. Strict adherence to religious dictates did not trump his historical mission. What does the Hindu custom and religion say? To become Muslim is to lose Dharma. To forsake Dharma is like death. How is it possible to bring the dead back to life? If you commit a sin in this life, you cannot be reborn as a human in the next life. You would be born an insect. This is what the Hindu *Dharmashastras* tell us. In

~ 85 ~

Shivaji's time, the interpretation of the *Dharmashastras* was much harsher. Shivaji was not held by these conventions. He reconverted Hindus who had embraced Islam, and he established relations through marriage with them. Shivaji did not feel that if they had rejected Hinduism, they should be seen as outcastes.

Bajaji Nimbalkar and Netaji Palkar converted to Islam. After ten years as Muslims, they reconverted to Hinduism. Shivaji's daughter married the son of Bajaji Nimbalkar (who was known as the "short one," since he was circumcised). Netaji Palkar, who lived in Afghanistan for eight years, reconverted to Hinduism in the presence of Shivaji. This approach to religion had been rejected under the rule of the Peshwas. Society had become so parochial that even the bravest of Peshwas, Bajirao, could not convert his own son, Samsher Bahadur, whose mother was Mastani (a Muslim). Bajirao could not even call his son Krishnarao. It was Bajirao who had to leave his family.

Were these two Hinduisms, one of Shivaji and the other of the Peshwas, the same religion? Shivaji had made the "untouchables" and Mahars chiefs of his forts. In Peshwai the "untouchables" were made to tie brooms to their waist so that the roads they walked on were automatically swept. They were forced to hang earthen pot around their neck so that the roads did not become impure by their spittoon. Was Shivaji's Hindu religion the same as the Peshwa's Hindu religion? Which of these two versions of Hindu religion does the *Senapati* [Bal Thackeray], who has taken upon himself the task of uniting the Hindus, want to establish?

Shivaji opposed superstition. It was believed that if a child was born upside down (his stomach to the ground), then it was inauspicious. Shivaji's son, Rajaram, was born in this manner. Everybody was dumbstruck. None would show their happiness at the childbirth. Shivaji heard this. He said, "It is symbolic. My son is born upside down. It means he will turn the empire upside down."

Faith is one thing. Superstition and fundamentalism are quite another.

Distortion of History

SHIVAJI — AN INCARNATION?

Was Shivaji an incarnation of god? A large number of people believe this to be true. Some call him Shiva's incarnation; others, an incarnation of Vishnu. It does not take long in our country for humans to become gods. We even have a term for it. *Dev manoos* — godlike person. We treat anyone who is great in any respect, including those who do the people's welfare, as god. Is this an instance of the simple faith in god or is it the cunning of some people who have malicious intent?

Did Shivaji's contemporaries turn him into an avatar, an incarnation? We cannot be sure. But we do know that they attributed miraculous powers to him, such as flight and invisibility. Of course these are false. Shivaji would have benefited from these rumours, since they would have increased his followers' loyalty. But there is a difference between the calculated promotion of ignorance and history.

Shivaji was a human being. He was a good and great man. Shivaji had intelligence and foresight, he was a pragmatic man of morals. He was a brave and great warrior. But he was human. He was not a god. He was not an avatar.

What are the consequences of turning Shivaji into a god? If he is made into a god, then we get away from our responsibility to emulate him. If someone says, "Behave like

Shivaji: don't trouble the *ryots*; don't touch the stem of *ryot's* crops; don't shield the rapists; love your religion, but do not hate the religion of others," then here comes the reply — How can we compare ourselves with Shivaji? He was god's avatar — we are only human. How can we hope to behave like him? We will behave the way we can. As Shivaji is only a god, it is enough to worship his image once a year, to only celebrate his birth anniversary, collect donations in his name, spend some of it on some program and gobble the rest, actually to spend very little and misappropriate most of it, arrange processions, apply *tilak* to our foreheads — this is all. One calls oneself a *Shivabhakta,* and hopes to garner influence. However one does not feel obliged to follow Shivaji's example. Shivaji came to *ryots'* help. Do these hypocrite *bhaktas* help the *ryots*? Actually they make use of Shivaji's name to threaten people. Shivaji's portrait and his flag are raised aloft on illicit distilleries, gambling dens and such similar activities. This is a misuse of Shivaji. We must understand who Shivaji was and put a stop to this misuse. We must understand who Shivaji was so that we can distinguish between his true followers and the hypocrites.

SHIVAJI AND THE BHAWANI SWORD

Did Shivaji succeed because he wielded the Bhavani Talwar, a sword blessed by Goddess Bhavani? A Chief Minister of Maharashtra tried to become popular in recent years by his quest to retrieve the sword from the Royal Collection in London.

Researchers have shown that the Bhavani Talwar was made in Portugal, where the techniques to forge swords from various metals was very advanced. The Portuguese brought this sword to Goa, from where it went to Sawants, and then to Shivaji. Mother Bhavani did not play a role in the forging of the sword. In Satara, there is a sword in a museum that some say was used by Shivaji. There is an ongoing dispute as to whether this is the Bhavani Talwar. On that sword, there is an inscription in Portuguese. Anyone can see that.

Those who use the people's ignorance and their faith to push their own agenda are not prepared to let people know the truth. It is not possible to understand the real Shivaji and Mother Bhawani by shouting Jai-Shivaji and Jai-Bhawani every morning and evening.

PHONY FOLLOWERS

Great heroes are again and again subjected to a tragedy. When these heroic individuals are alive, people in power oppose them. They oppose their principles and the work that they undertake. They even try to kill them and to obliterate their work. Unfortunately for them, they do not always succeed in destroying the greatness of such individuals. Common people accept them when they are alive and their ideas when they are dead. They try to emulate them.

Those who oppose such heroic individuals play a clever trick. They themselves become the hero's ardent devotees. They worship the hero, celebrate the hero's anniversaries, build temples, and print portraits. While doing this, they play a subtle trick. They distort the mission to improve the people's welfare, trying hard to erase this history. They take great care that their antiestablishment views do not reach the masses. They see that their teachings of rebellion against the establishment do not reach the oppressed. They deceive people—they write false history. They teach false history. They sell adulterated history, adroitly mixing truth with a lot of untruth. They utilize the antiestablishment ideology to reinforce their own conservative position. These charlatans, under the garb of the leaders of society, pick up the images and symbols that people revere. They distort those symbols and images and destroy their very core. The established people are very clever. Some are established because they have power; some because they possess wealth; some because they have social status. In fact, they are all one.

Dnyaneshwar (1275-1296) brought knowledge from Sanskrit to Prakrit, the people's language. He attacked the monopoly of the handful, freeing knowledge toward the people. He described a buffalo reciting the Vedas, with the buffalo standing in for the illiterate. Dnyaneshwar offered them knowledge in a language they could understand. He rebelled against the monopolists of knowledge. The elite persecuted him — calling his siblings offspring of *sanyasis*, they outcaste them. They refused to perform their *maunji bandhan* (Dnyaneshwar did not have millions of gold coins or encounter a Gaga Bhatta, both of which allowed Shivaji to have his coronation performed). Dnyaneshwar took *sanjeevan samadhi* (to be buried alive) at a very young age. Did this really happen?

When he died, the cultural, religious and socio-economic heirs of the people who persecuted Dnyaneshwar started to sing his eulogies. They proclaimed that history has not seen any other person as great as Dnyaneshwar. They chanted his name day and night, while denying the common people the right to knowledge. The fate of Dnyaneshwar is not uncommon even in the divine realm — the saints themselves are said to have boycotted their fellow saint, Chakradhar, for introducing the texts in Prakrit.

Tukaram (1608-1649) faced persecution from Mambaji. They drowned his *abhangs* and his *Gatha* — his devotional poetry — in the Indrayani River. What they did to him is unclear, but they spread a wild rumour that he went, body and soul, directly to *vaikuntha*, the heavenly abode. Films of Tukaram's life often show an airplane taking him to heaven! But even after they drowned Tukaram's *abhangs* in the river, they remained with the people who went on singing them. When the heirs of Mambaji saw that even after drowning his *abhangs* and after sending Tukaram to heaven they could not finish him off, they began to eulogise him. They interpolated their own *abhangs* into his authentic *abhangs*. They began to sing *kirtans* and tell stories based on them. They played the regular tricks of power. They took care that the whiplash that Tukaram had used against superstition and injustice did not reach the masses.

Do we need to go that far in the past to make our point? What did they do to Mahatma Gandhi? They conspired and assassinated him. Some who took part in the conspiracy escaped by guile. Some were hanged. Now they say, "a mad man killed Gandhiji." Were the conspirators lunatics? When Mahatma Gandhi was assassinated, sweets were distributed and consumed with glee in many quarters. Nathuram Godse was felicitated as a martyr. Now what do Nathuram Godse's colleagues and followers say? They cheekily claim that they have adopted Gandhi's ideology, supplemented with socialism! When they saw that Gandhi could not be finished, they pretended to be his followers. It was their way of truly finishing him off.

IF SHIVAJI WERE TO APPEAR TODAY ...

Shivaji's life and legacy have been distorted for a very long time. The distortion continues with renewed vigour.

Shivaji despised feudal rights, and refused to dole out privy privileges. Today's Shivabhaktas create newer and newer privileges for the rich. They tell the modern princes and feudal prodigals to do whatever they want in their dominions. Loot the *ryots*! Drink and amuse yourselves! What we need from you is to support us so that we can run the "government." Then, we can also loot the *ryots*. It is true that there are no principalities of the old type today, but new principalities have emerged and grow in strength and number. Sugar barons are the new princes in one set of districts. Government departments and state power have also been turned into fiefs, passed on from generation to generation.

Democracy calls for the decentralization of power. But decentralization does not mean that power be inherited within a set of families. These new feudal lords exploit and oppress the *ryots* more than they did at Shivaji's times. If a *ryot* dares to go against the interests of a sugar baron, he is finished. He does not get any loan, does not get fertilizers, his sugarcane is kept drying in the field. He eats dust within two years; others look at him, learn a "proper lesson" and refrain from daring the baron. The baron becomes invincible.

Don't these new barons and princes cast their evil eye

on innocent daughters of the *ryot*? Don't rapes take place? Hasn't the *ryot* been emaciated in serving and entertaining these modern princes in Shivaji's Maharashtra where the *ryots'* Raja had always insisted that not a single stem of *ryot's* crop would be harmed in his state?

All this happens shouting *Shivaji Maharaj ki Jai* ("Hail Shivaji"). Is it not a shame? What if Shivaji himself was present to see all this? What would he do? Of course he is not present. He can't be present. But don't we have his teachings with us? The true way of remembering Shivaji is to abolish these new princes.

Today Hindu-Muslim riots are taking place in Shivaji's name. We must tell these religious fanatics that Shivaji himself was not fanatic. He had faith in Hindu religion; but he did not hate Islam. He believed in god but he was not superstitious. Just as Hindus have rioters among them, there are rioters among Muslims as well. They too have their own religious fanatics. Some Muslims believe that they are heirs of some Shehanshah. They think that once they were the rulers of this country. They forget that even when Muslim kings were ruling all the Muslims were not eating only biryani and drinking fine liquor. The majority of Muslims were very poor. But what about those who spilled their blood, who sacrificed their life for *Swaraj*? Were they not your forefathers? Who does one choose to stand with — Aurangzeb and Adil Shah or Madari Mehtar, Ibrahim Khan, Daulat Khan and Kazi Hyder? Shivaji's *Swaraj* was not for Hindus alone. It was equally for the Muslims in Maharashtra.

Jai Bhavani, Jai Shivaji is used to attack both Muslims and *dalits*. The new followers of Shivaji oppose reservations for *dalits*. They conveniently forget that Shivaji had consciously enrolled *dalits* into service. He had given them prestige.

There is a tendency to distort the legacy of heroes. It does not happen unintentionally. Some might originate in ignorance, but most of it is a product of deliberate mischief. It is done to serve some vested interests. Whatever the difference, the consequences are the same.

What have they — the powerful — done to Shivaji? Have they made Shivaji bigger or smaller during the last fifty years? What has happened in terms of his acceptance across the regions? Has it grown or lessened? Fifty years ago his portraits used to be displayed outside Maharashtra. They were displayed in Madhya Pradesh. They were put up in Karnataka in the South. They were hung in Baroda and Gujarat. During the Samyukta Maharashtra Movement we all woke up to the Maharashtrian identity taking inspiration from Shivaji. Of course, the movement of Samyukta Maharashtra for a linguistic Marathi state was quite justified. It was certainly justified to politically remember Shivaji as he had prepared a Rajya Bhasha Kosha. However we did not observe the limits of propriety. One of the stalwarts of the Samyukta Maharashtra Movement used to say in speeches, "Maharashtra has History whereas others have Geography only!" Of course, it used to evoke a tremendous applause. This was extremism. Shivaji is dear to Maharashtra. Just as Maharashtra has the history of Shivaji, doesn't Karnataka have the history of Rani Channamma? Doesn't Rajasthan have Rana Pratap's history? Are the states of Madhya Pradesh and Gujarat of recent origin? True, a sense of propriety was lost in the heat of propaganda. Finally we succeeded in making Samyukta Maharashtra. However, we, at the same time, put Shivaji in the confines of the walls of Maharashtra.

Shivaji, who was also popular outside, was made to belong to Maharashtra alone.

What is now happening in Maharashtra? The Shiv Sena was founded in the 1960s. This party invokes Shivaji's name in whatever it does, against non-Maharashtrians or against Muslims. These forces have founded many more outfits: Hindu Ekta, Maratha Maha Sangh, Patit Pawan Sanghatana — all these chant Shivaji's name. Shivaji, who belonged to the whole of Maharashtra, is now made to represent the Maharashtrian Hindus alone. He is turned into a *Go-Brahman Pratipalak*. Maratha Maha Sangh makes him represent Marathas alone. When they opposed reservations, the slogan they raised was *Shivaji Maharaj ki Jai*. When *dalit* hamlets were attacked in Marathwada and elsewhere, again the slogan used was *Jai Shivaji, Jai Bhawani*. Thus Shivaji is turned into a caste Hindu. He was brought into the fold of Brahmans, he was made to belong to 96 families, genuine or not, of Marathas. This is purely revisionist history of the elite.

Shivaji is cynically used to serve selfish interests. Something similar had happened at the time of World War II. The British wanted to enlist Indian youth to the armed services. They printed posters with Shivaji's picture on it, calling upon "You *mavlas* of Shivaji! Enlist today! Shivaji was brave; you too are brave. Join the War!" Those who had forced the country into slavery used Shivaji. Now those who are hell bent upon dividing the country, those who are dividing the poor *ryots* on the basis of caste and religion, are again using him.

It may be their business to do this. But why should we make it our own? Why should we allow them to do so? They propound a false history. They only shout *Jai*. We must recount the true history, not merely shout *Jai*. Those who are well off in terms of power, wealth, status and knowledge do not use force alone to maintain their hegemony. They do not use only weapons, truncheons and the state. They use ideas. They use history. They encourage such ideas amongst the people; they make them digest the philosophy and the history which is useful to maintain their own superiority. Such thought and philosophy, such false, half true and distorted history, help to maintain the *status quo*. Thought is a very effective weapon. It lasts a very long time. It is superior to the gun. The rulers always use this weapon against the oppressed.

Those who have something to lose — power and wealth — use all the weapons of the privileged to safeguard their authority. Those who have nothing to lose — who are dispossessed, need to sharpen the weapon of their ideology. Change is not possible without ideas, without thoughts. This is the reason why the *ryots* today must fathom Shivaji's history. It should be interpreted in a meaningful way. Whatever is worthless in history must be consigned to the dustbin. Whatever is valuable must be examined properly. New progressive ideas must be added to them. Such new updated ideas must be carried over to the next stage of history.

There is a lot in Shivaji's history, his ideas, and his practice; there is much in the inspiring forces behind his cause and achievements. All this can be extremely beneficial to today's *ryots*. We must understand all this properly and take it ahead.

APPENDIX

Shivaji's Letters

LETTER NO. 1.
TO JUMLEDARS, HAVALDARS AND
CLERKS OF CHIPLUN

19th May 1673
Shri Bhavani Shankar

The Royal army was to camp in the Province of Chiplun. Food grains and other goods were stored at Dabhol as reserves for the monsoon. However, these were supplied to the army. All the grains and hay was spent on the maintenance of the army. As a consequence, the ryots suffered a great deal. Moreover, because of the summer, the cavalry too had to camp. We tried to meet the expenses by borrowing money from the Clerk and from various forts. If you do not utilize these resources judiciously, if you go on squandering them listlessly they will soon be exhausted and you will end up without food in pouring rains; you will starve and the horses will start dying. It will mean that you have been responsible for their death. Then you may end up causing trouble to the ryots. Some of you will extract grains from peasants, some bread, some hay, some firewood and some vegetables. If you resort to such acts, whoever of the peasants have stayed back to save themselves from loot and oppression will at once start leaving. Many will starve to death. It will mean that you are worse than the Mughal invaders! The ryots will curse you! The whole blame will befall you. So you better understand this, whether you are a sepoy or a soldier, you must not burden the villagers with a leaf or a twig. We have provided from the royal treasury. Whatever one requires, be it food or hay for cattle or firewood or vegetables: go to the bazaars and buy whatever you need. There is no need to apply force on anyone to feed you. The supplies must be utilized economically so that they suffice for the entire monsoon. Take as much ration as is being supplied by clerks; use it in such a way that no one starves and that the horses grow healthy day by day. There is no need to threaten the clerks, demanding from them anything at will, and attacking or looting the stores or warehouses. As you are aware, these are the days of summer and soldiers are camping in wooden houses. Some are likely to light bonfires, some will set up ovens at wrong places, some will want to light tobacco. Hay is strewn around. If anybody is not careful when the wind is blowing, it may cause a great disaster. Once a house catches fire, it will spread to other houses as well. If the tiniest of cinders touches a straw, fire will engulf all the hay around. After this, whether you behead peasants or threaten the clerks there will not be any wood left to build any more places for your camp. Everyone must understand this. Therefore, all those responsible are hereby ordered that they take rounds, that they take care so that fire does not break as a result of bonfires, ovens and wicks of lamps as mice are apt to take away the burning wicks. Everything possible must be done to protect hay. It will ensure the survival of the horses through the rains. If this is not done, there will be no horses to look after, no horses to be fed. No cavalry!

You will be without the burden of looking after them! This is the reason why I have written in detail. All those important Jumledars, Havaldars and Clerks are to hereby pay proper heed to this detail. You are all to be on your toes. You are all to collect proper information and act accordingly. Anyone who ignores this, anyone who makes a mistake, will defame the name of Maratha. How is he, then, to get employment? Nobody shall deviate from this because none shall be spared.

LETTER NO. 2
TO SUBEDAR ON REVENUE

5th September 1676
Shri Shankar
Greetings from Rajashri Shivaji Raja to Ramaji Anant Subedar of Prebhavali Province.

You have been serving the State with honesty and without defrauding it. Similarly, you are expected to look after the cultivation of crops, from sowing to harvesting, without a desire for personal gains. There is crop-sharing observed all over the state. Shares of the tenants and the State should be properly divided. If the ryots are tricked in any manner you shall face royal displeasure. It is not my order that money be collected from the ryots. You are not supposed to collect money to the value of food grains. You must collect our share of grains themselves. Those are to be later sold for a better price. The State should profit from such a sale. All the tax in kind must be collected on the basis of the yields. It should be then properly stored and sold in proper season. The whole transaction should be planned in such a manner that the goods should be sold at proper time and at a high price only and there must not be any waste either. You must sell, in this fashion, coconut, betel nut, pepper etc. If you sell goods at a profit at ten bazaars, you will also get a proper benefit from it. The ryots should be empowered and you should help them in planting crops. For this you must take great efforts and visit every village. You should call all the tenants in the village together and identify who can cultivate which and how much land depending upon their ability to put in human labour and other capacities. There may be those who are handicapped because they do not possess bullocks, plough, or food to eat. They should be paid cash enough to buy a pair of bullocks and grains to eat. Let them till the land as much as they can. No interest should be charged on this loan and only capital amount should be collected from them as and when they are in a condition of repaying. I shall not object even if you have to spend about two lacs on this. Only you must ensure that the money thus spent reaches the beneficiary and that all fallow land is brought under cultivation. This encourages the peasant to work more. He is exempted from paying whatever he owes to the treasury due to losses that he has suffered. Report to your senior officer on these matters and he will issue the proper order of exemption. I am sure you will perform your duty with proper care and discretion.

LETTER NO. 3
TO AURANGZEB ABOUT JAZIYA TAX

Circa 1657
From Shivaji, True to His Words, to Aurangzeb
I had to leave, due to a quirk of Destiny, without a farewell. . . .

After our return we heard that the Emperor's treasury has become empty. It is also learnt that the government of the Empire is running its daily administration by collecting *jaziya* from Hindus. In fact, formerly, Emperor Akbar ruled with great equanimity for fifty-two years. Therefore, apart from the Daudis and Mohammedis, the religious practices of Hindus such as Brahmans and Shevades were protected. The Emperor helped these religions. Therefore, he was hailed as a Jagatguru. This ensured success to him in all the endeavours that he undertook. He conquered land after land. After him Emperor Nuruddin Jehangir ruled for twenty-two years with the blessings of the Almighty and went to the heaven. Shah Jahan too ruled for thirty-two years. They were brave Emperors and earned great respect. They established many new practices. They too were capable of levying the *jaziya*. But all, small and big, follow their own religion and are God's children. In spite of all this they never resorted to injustice. Even now all sing in their praise. All, big and small, feel blessed by them. One reaps as one sows. Those Emperors had always their eyes fixed on people's welfare. Now, under your rule, you have lost many forts and provinces. The rest are also likely to be lost. This is because you do not spare in doing everything that is base. The ryots have become miserable. None of the revenue divisions is paying you even one per cent of its total produce. Even the Emperor and his progeny are living in impoverished condition. It is therefore not hard to imagine under what conditions the other lords must be living. In sum, soldiers are frustrated, merchants are howling and Muslims are crying. Hindus burn from within. Several cannot get sufficient food to eat. Is this governance? Over and above all this, there is *jaziya*. The word has spread east and west, far and wide, that the Emperor of Hindustan levies *jaziya* on Fakirs, Brahmans, Shevades, Jogis, Sanyasis, Bairagis, poor and miserable. The Emperor takes pride in this and even surpasses Emperor Timur's deeds. The Quran is a Heavenly Book. It is God's utterance. It commands that God belongs to all Muslims and, in fact, the entire world. Good or bad, both are God's creation. In masjids, it is He who is prayed. In temples, it is He for whom the bells are tolled. To oppose anyone's religion is like forsaking one's own religion. It is wiping out what God wrote; it is to blame God Himself. You should therefore discriminate between good and bad. This is all the more necessary as defaming matter is like defaming the Creator of matter Himself. *Jaziya* can in no way be called just. Sultan Ahmed Gujrathi ruled in this manner and soon bit dust. Those who are made to suffer injustice finally blow out smoke through their mouth hotter than even the fire that burns the Devil. The perpetrator burns out faster than the Devil himself. So it is advisable that the soiled mind is washed sooner than later. Above all this, if you feel that the true religion is in persecuting Hindus, you should first collect the *jaziya* from Raja Jai Singh. Others will easily follow suit. The poor are like ants and gnats. There is nothing heroic in persecuting them. It is very surprising to see that even loyal ones blatantly try to hide fire under hay. So be it. Let the Sun of the Empire shine bright from the Eastern Mountains of Heroism.

References

Bedekar, D.K., *Samyukta Maharashtra*, Chitrashala Press, Pune, 1947

Bhagwat, Rajaramshastri, *Marathyasambandhiche Char Bol*

Dange, S.A., *Bara Bhashane*, Abhinav Prakashan; Mumbai, 1975

Deshpande, P.N., *Shivaji Maharajanchi Patre*

Gadkari, Jayant, *Shivaji: Lok Kalyankari Raja*

Godse, D.G., *Sammade Talash*, Popular Prakashan, Mumbai, 1980

———, *Shakti Saushthav*, Popular Prakashan, Mumbai, 1978

Joshi, Sharad, et al., *Shetkaryancha Raja Shivaji*, Shetkari Prakashan, Raigadh

Kale, D.V., *Chhatrapati Shivaji Maharaj*, Pune Vidyapeeth, Pune, 1961

Keluskar, A.A., *Shri Chhatrapati Shivaji Maharaj Yanche Charitra*

Kulkarni, A.R., *Shivkalin Maharashtra*, Shivaji University, Kolhapur, 1977

Kurundkar, Narhar, *Shivaji Maharajanche Jeevan Rahasya*

Madhavrao, Pagadi Setu, *Chhatrapati Shivaji*, Continental Prakashan, Pune, 1974

Pendse, Lalji, *Dharma ki Kranti*, Lalji Pendse, Mumbai, 1942

Rajwade, V.K., *Aitihasik Prastavana*, Chitrashala Press, Pune

Ranade, M.G., *The Rise of Maratha Power*, Punalekar and Sons, Bombay, 1902

Sardar, G.B., *Sant Vangmayachi Samajik Phalashruti*.

Sardesai, G.S., *Shakakarta Shivaji*, K. B. Dhavale, Mumbai, 1935

Sarkar, Jadu Nath, *Shivaji and his Times*, Orient Longman, Delhi, 1973

Sen, S.N., *The Administrative System of Marathas*, Calcutta, 1925

Shejwalkar, T.S., *Shivcharitra — Prastavana va Arakhada*, Maratha Mandir, Mumbai, 1964

PRABHAT PATNAIK

AFTERWORD

One of the Finest

I was based in Trivandrum at the time, working in the Kerala State Planning Board. I got a call one day from Kolhapur from Govind Pansare of the Communist Party of India, asking me if I would give the annual memorial lecture for that year, instituted in the memory of his son, Avinash, a CPI youth activist who had met an untimely death a few years earlier. I agreed, though I did not know Pansare. So, one morning I flew from Trivandrum to Mumbai, was met by some CPI activists who took me to the Bhupesh Gupta Bhavan of the party, located within a stone's throw of the Siddhivinayak temple in central Mumbai, to await the overnight train that would take me to Kolhapur.

Two memories of that evening are etched in my mind. One was the enormous ruckus made by a group of children on the top floor of the Bhupesh Gupta Bhavan where I was lodged. They were apparently rehearsing for a play. This, I was told, was a common practice: a part of the building was given for use everyday without any charge for various cultural activities by local children, a gesture on the party's part which impressed me greatly. The other memory is of the two CPI activists, who took me out for a walk before dropping me off at Dadar station, pointing out the telltale signs of Mumbai's transition from a fishing village to a megapolis; such signs, like old fishermen's huts, which had been built over subsequently but whose remnants had not been fully erased, abounded in that neighbourhood.

At Kolhapur, where I was lodged at the university guest house, I met Govind Pansare for the first time — a tall, impressive, grey-haired gentleman with great gravitas and a touching concern for my comfort, who was held in very high esteem by everyone around. At the venue of the lecture, scheduled for late afternoon, where I went after lunch, there was an *adda* going on with stories of Chhatrapati Shahu Maharaj and of Govind Pansare (he himself had not turned up) doing the rounds. Shahu remains an iconic figure for the social emancipation movement in the country, because he did much in his area to eliminate "untouchability" and other such oppressive social practices.

Apparently, Shahu had a novel way of doing so: he had once asked a person of dalit origin, who had come to him for assistance, to start a tea shop in Kolhapur for which he had provided financial help; and any of his "subjects" who wanted to meet him for any reason were asked to come in the morning to the tea shop where he would invariably be ensconced having tea, together with his ministers and advisors, much against the latter's wishes. The visitor would be gracefully offered tea by Shahu that he could scarcely refuse. Hence everyone perforce was made to drink tea prepared by a dalit because nobody dared to incur the displeasure of the ruler. And this was around the beginning of the 20th century!

At that *adda* I also learned of Comrade Pansare's background and his fight against casteist and fundamentalist tendencies in western Maharashtra. Coming from an extremely impecunious family, Pansare had educated himself with great difficulty, taking up the job of a peon for some time to finance his studies. He had been drawn to the communist movement in his student days, and after some years of working as an academic in a local college, had decided to become a full-time party activist, doing trade union work and organizing the oppressed in the region. He had risen to become the Maharashtra state secretary of the CPI and had held a number of important positions in the party. But he had always been of the view that the communist movement had to engage itself with the struggle for social emancipation, for which an ideological fight against reactionary positions had to be incessantly carried out.

It was this conviction that had prompted him to write a number of path-breaking books, including, above all, this one on Shivaji in which he had portrayed the latter not as an upholder of Hinduism, as is usually done, nor even as a mere "backward caste" leader asserting himself against Brahmanical dominance, but as a "secular" ruler who pioneered a Welfare State. He had written: "Shivaji had not become popular because he was just a Hindu king, but because his priority was welfare of the common people. He fought for justice, ensured security to women, and recruited fighters irrespective of their caste and community to help the dream of Swarajya come true." This book, translated into many languages, has sold over one lakh copies. I am pleased that it is now being brought out by LeftWord in this edition.

Pansare's book is based on a speech he delivered in May

1987. It portrayed Shivaji not only as socially progressive, but also as a rationalist. The promotion of rational thought was centrally important to Pansare. When Narendra Dabholkar, the president of the Maharashtra Andhashraddha Nirmoolan Samiti was assassinated in 2013, its membership turned to Pansare to take over its leadership. Dabholkar had drafted the Anti-Superstition and Black Magic Act, which had been promulgated as an ordinance four days after his murder and finally passed by the legislature on December 13, 2013. Pansare had fully backed this bill. He had received a letter that had warned, "*Tumcha Dabholkar karen*" ("You will meet Dabholkar's fate"). It did not stop Pansare.

The event at Kolhapur that evening in the memory of Avinash Pansare was very well-attended; there must have been several hundred people in the audience. Even more impressive was the stack of questions in written form that was submitted to me to answer at the end of my lecture. In fact, the stack was so large that before I could come anywhere near its end, I was whisked off to the railway station to ensure that I did not miss the train back to Mumbai.

In television studio discussions in Delhi, both hosts and guests appear generally agreed that the Left in India has become largely inconsequential, a spent force; and this view is echoed in the print and social media. But whether in Jullundur or Kolhapur or Rohtak or Guwahati or Tirunelveli, literally hundreds of persons regularly make it a point to attend serious intellectual discussions organized by the Left. Hence, only someone exclusively and myopically focused on parliamentary election results, someone who does not appreciate the power of ideas, who does not understand the fact that ideas, to borrow Mao Zedong's phrase, can become a "material force", can hold the view that the Left is a spent force. For me, that evening in Kolhapur once more brought home this lesson.

Arriving back at the Dadar station next morning, I got into an auto-rickshaw to take me to the Bhupesh Gupta Bhavan, but to my chagrin, the driver would not budge. At that hour of the morning, several people, including large numbers of women of different ages, go to the Siddhivinayak temple to offer flowers; so, auto-rickshaws are never available at that time for single occupants. Each carries at least four passengers, and each passenger pays a fixed amount for being transported to the temple. I, therefore, had to suppress my "bourgeois" desire to have an auto-rickshaw all to myself and to wait until three other devotees had joined me. Sandwiched between them, I made the journey to the temple, paying some absurdly trivial sum, and then walked the short distance to the Bhupesh Gupta Bhavan.

After getting ready and consuming a *masala dosa* at a dhaba nearby, I took a taxi, all to myself, to Santa Cruz airport, where I had to catch a flight to Calcutta for carrying out some official work relating to academic administration. Since the work at Calcutta was "official", I was met by a chauffeur-driven car at the airport and taken to what I suppose was a five-star hotel, all of which was a complete contrast to my Mumbai sojourn. Throughout that day, however, the memory of Govind Pansare and his wife, Uma, kept coming back to me.

That memory came back to me again last February when I read in the papers that Govind Pansare and Uma Pansare had been shot at while taking a morning walk near their house in Kolhapur and that he had succumbed to his injuries in the hospital. Even though the exact identity of his assailants was not known, the general view was that it was some extremist Hindutva group. Pansare had been threatened earlier for his rationalist work. A few days before his assassination, he had given a spirited talk at Shivaji University, where he had criticized Nathuram Godse, Gandhi's assassin. Criticism of Godse who is enjoying a revival of sorts in the new atmosphere of right-wing hegemony, had been impossible to stomach for the Hindu Right. Sanathan Sanstha, a right-wing group, had filed a defamation charge against Pansare. He had been openly threatened by them. Pansare died like Dabholkar — both on their morning walk, both killed by men on motorcycles.

Whatever freedom we enjoy in this country, whatever "modernity" we have in this country, whatever social equality we have achieved in this country, is continuously under attack, and its preservation is made possible by the continuous struggles undertaken by a large number of persons scattered all over India. They do not make it to New Delhi's TV studios, they are not to be found in the corridors of power in the nation's capital, and they do not even belong to the metropolitan centres of the country. But, because of their sheer dedication, indefatigable energy and unquestionable integrity, they wield great influence among the people in their respective regions, in spite of the overwhelming odds stacked against them.

Among all such persons, Govind Pansare was undoubtedly one of the finest.

GOVIND PANSARE

(26 November 1933 – 20 February 2015) was one of Maharashtra's leading Communist leaders and public intellectuals. Starting out in the Rashtra Seva Dal, he joined the Communist Party of India in 1952, and went on to become its Maharashtra State Secretary, as well as a member of the party's National Executive. An active trade unionist, he was also a labour lawyer. Pansare took part in many social reform movements in Maharashtra, including movements against superstition and for inter-caste marriage. He was a prolific writer and speaker, and authored at least ten books, including the bestselling *Shivaji Kon Hota?*

ANIRUDH DESHPANDE

is Associate Professor, Department of History, University of Delhi, Delhi. He is co-editor, along with Partha Sarathi Gupta, of *The British Raj and its Indian Armed Forces, 1857-1939* (2002), and author of *British Military Policy in India 1900-1945: Colonial Constraints and Declining Power* (2005), *Class, Power and Consciousness in Indian Cinema and Television* (2009), *A Spring of Despair: Mutiny, Rebellion and Death in India, 1946* and *Cinema Aur Itihaas – Kuch Paraspar Sambandh* (both forthcoming).

PRABHAT PATNAIK

retired as Professor, Centre for Economic Studies and Planning, Jawaharlal Nehru University, New Delhi in 2010. He was the Vice-Chairman of the Kerala State Planning Board, 2006-2011. One of India's best-known Marxist intellectuals, Patnaik is the author of *Time, Inflation and Growth* (1988), *Economics and Egalitarianism* (1990), *Whatever Happened to Imperialism and Other Essays* (1995), *Accumulation and Stability Under Capitalism* (1997), *The Retreat to Unfreedom* (2003), *The Value of Money* (2008) and *Re-envisioning Socialism* (2011).

UDAY NARKAR

is the translator of several books from English to Marathi and vice-versa. He taught at the Yashwantrao Chavan College, Kolhapur, for 16 years, and was a senior producer in ETV-Marathi for 4 years. Since then he has been a full time worker of the CPI(M) and is currently Secretary, Kolhapur District Committee and member of the Maharashtra State Committee of the party.